FRANKEL

THE WONDER HORSE

FRANKEL

THE WONDER HORSE

edited by
ANDREW PENNINGTON

with a Foreword by
SIR PETER O'SULLEVAN

RACING POST

First published in Great Britain in 2012 by
Racing Post Books
Axis House, Compton, Newbury, Berkshire, RG20 6NL

10 9 8 7 6 5 4 3 2

A catalogue record for this book is available from the British Library.

ISBN 978-1-908216-63-2

All the photographs in this book are from the *Racing Post*, with the
exception of those on pages 23 and 185 (Mark Cranham); 31, 70, 98
(lower) and 184 (Getty Images); 43 (Juddmonte Farms); 46–7 and 50
(Steven Cargill); and 73 and 138 (Dan Abraham).

Designed by Soapbox
www.soapbox.co.uk

Printed and bound in the UK by Butler, Tanner and Dennis, Frome

Every effort has been made to fulfil requirements with regard to
copyright material. The author and publisher will be glad to rectify
any omissions at the earliest opportunity.

www.racingpost.com/shop

Contents

Foreword

by Sir Peter O'Sullevan CBE

At the top of Mount Olympus, home of the gods, Frankel filled his lungs – and with his heart and respiratory functions enhanced by altitude, descended to spend three unforgettable racing years with ordinary mortals, and to beguile us with his power.

The gods had dictated that he would be blessed in having around him the ideal connections.

Prince Khalid Abdulla has been a major player in world racing long enough to know the importance of patience when owning a champion – and that patience has been mirrored in Frankel's groom Sandeep Gauravaram and work rider Shane Fetherstonhaugh.

Tom Queally's devotion to Frankel was combined with a proper thoughtfulness towards the horse's legion of fans, never better illustrated than when he took the colt all the way down the course after the Champion Stakes to receive the appreciation of the crowd.

And most of all, Sir Henry Cecil – a man with 'green fingers' with horses as much as in his beloved rose garden – transmuted Frankel from the fizzy juvenile to the mature four-year-old so laid back that he was stealing a brief nap when the Ascot stalls opened.

One sight on that magical October afternoon will remain with me for ever: Her Majesty the Queen giving an enthusiastic wave – more like a young girl's wave of delight than the more formal royal version – as Tom Queally brought Frankel past the Royal Box after the race. That wave seemed to sum up the human response to an equine immortal.

I leave it to others to engage in debate about just where Frankel stands in the pantheon of great racehorses. Let's just be satisfied with the proposition that there's never been a better racehorse, and relish recollection of the racing days we have been privileged to enjoy with this heavenly horse.

This book, which combines wonderful photographs with the immediacy of *Racing Post* reportage of each of Frankel's races, is the perfect medium through which to relive the career of a true equine god.

Preface

by Andrew Pennington

This book charts the unparalleled career of Frankel, considered by many to be the greatest racehorse ever, through the words and pictures of the *Racing Post*'s award-winning writers and photographers.

The performances of Frankel shone like a beacon during his three years of racing, and the *Racing Post* was there every step of the way – from his debut on a wet summer's evening on Newmarket's July Course to his final performance at Ascot on British Champions Day.

I have used the *Post*'s experts and the paper's vast database to demonstrate Frankel's transcendence, while Graham Dench, editor of the *Form Book*, has written a bespoke analysis of each race to give a retrospective look at Frankel's running, and has also contributed 'The Raceform View' (page 206) to put Frankel into historical perspective.

One of the most eye-catching aspects of Frankel's career has been his speed and acceleration, so the *Racing Post* 'Topspeed' expert Dave Edwards has picked out four of the colt's most impressive performances on the clock and analysed those displays through his own stopwatch and through data supplied by TurfTrax.

These two sets of analyses will, it is hoped, demonstrate why Frankel is considered one of the all-time greats.

This project could not have been completed without a number of people: Sean Magee and Liz Ampairee, who have been of invaluable assistance during the whole project and to whom I am indebted; Rachel Bray at Soapbox for her design expertise; Edward Whitaker for his stunning pictures of Frankel's career (as well as Steven Cargill for the pictures from Frankel's debut at Newmarket on pages 46–7 and 50, and Dan Abraham for the photographs on pages 73 and 138); Graham Dench, Dave Edwards, Nancy Sexton and Brough Scott for writing specifically for the book; and other *Racing Post* writers for their on-the-spot dispatches.

And finally my grateful thanks to Frankel himself, the like of whom I will probably not see again during my lifetime.

Connections

The owner:
Prince Khalid Abdulla

Despite having been one of the major players in world horseracing, Prince Khalid Abdulla, owner and breeder of Frankel, has always maintained a quiet and self-effacing public profile. In June 2010 he gave a rare interview to **Brough Scott** *for the* Racing Post, *a few days after the Derby had been won for the third time in the famous green, pink and white colours – this time by Workforce – and two months before a highly promising homebred colt named Frankel made his racecourse debut. The result was a highly revealing insight into a remarkable man.*

Prince Khalid Abdulla was amused by the memories. 'You need to be lucky,' he says, as if this could explain the 30 years of glittering success crowned by Workforce's Derby last Saturday. 'This year, for example, I have won two Classics with Special Duty while being second.' The prince's smile is a slow one – but he likes it that way.

Courtesy should never be confused with softness, nor shyness with lack of will. For two hours in Paris on Thursday morning, Prince Khalid talked of a racing passion first lit when friends took him to Longchamp back in 1956. Never once did the courtesy or the self-effacing shyness slip, yet neither did the impression alter that the unique achievements of the prince's international Juddmonte empire still depend on having this remarkable owner-breeder at the heart of it all.

'But I know nothing about racing,' he says to the suggestion that he might have an input into a horse's programme. 'How can I tell a trainer what to do? I have very good people and good managers. I talk to them all the time. It is not a business but it is my only hobby and so we have to run it like a business – not to make money, but to make sure we control it.'

As he talks, the words – quiet and carefully chosen – are spoken in still-quite accented English and you think how far he is from, and yet how close he remains in his enthusiasm to, the thousands who also have racing as their thing.

He is sitting in the silk-lined ante-room at the top of the stairs in his town house on the edge of the elegant

Henry Cecil and Prince Khalid Abdulla at Newbury on Greenham Stakes day, 2011

Parc Monceau, not half a mile from the Bois de Boulogne and Longchamp, ready to go to lunch with important visitors from his native Saudi Arabia. Yet he will return in time to watch a once-raced Oasis Dream colt called Uphold wing home at 3-1 in the second division of the maiden race at Nottingham. Punters in betting shops who blindly back the pink and green will be just as pleased as a prince in Paris – especially those who got the early 7-1.

Uphold's was a 20th British win of a season with a current total of £1.5 million prize-money already and which could yet eclipse all that has gone before. It is a far cry from those first thoroughbred sightings of 1956.

'I was only over here,' remembers Prince Khalid, 'because my oldest son needed treatment. But I had two Saudi friends and they used to go to the races every day. So instead of learning the French language, I started going with them.

'At that time, of course,' he adds with a slight dip of the head which acknowledges that financial matters are rather better now, 'I had not any money. But I promised myself that one day I would have a horse running in my colours at Longchamp.'

That initial dream was put on hold, but after completing his history studies in America and Riyadh, the prince – he is cousin and brother-in-law of King Abdulla of Saudi Arabia – started out in a business which was eventually to grow into the massive Mawared conglomerate. He now takes a back seat and leaves the running to his sons, but back in 1977 business was looking up and had taken him to London. 'I began to watch the races in England,' he says with relish, 'and I felt that the promise should be realised.'

At this stage the late Humphrey Cottrill and trainer Jeremy Tree should each take a posthumous bow. For it was into the bloodstock advisor's hands, and via him to Tree's stable, that Abdulla delivered himself with a vague wish that he wanted to buy some horses. Faced with this quiet, apparently naive but evidently very wealthy Saudi prince there are many in the racing game who would have greedily taken the short-term view and thus soured off one of the greatest individual benefactors in racing history. They didn't. The prince wanted to buy four horses. They said it was too many.

'Jeremy said we could do it with two horses,' recalls Prince Khalid, 'but I said that if we had at least four we might have some luck. None of them did win that first year, but Aliya won a Group race later, and of the ones we bought in 1978, Abeer won the Queen Mary Stakes. She was not expensive – 25,000gns I think.'

Others in that second year were quite a bit more costly, but while the 264,000gns shelled out for Sand Hawk was almost entirely wasted, the $225,000 that Cottrill and Tree paid at Keeneland for a bay colt by In Reality was very much not so. Named Known Fact, the colt won the 1979 Middle Park and was also victor, albeit on Nureyev's disqualification, of the 1980 2,000 Guineas. That success was the first leg of what would eventually become a clean sweep of the Classics in Britain and France for those green silks with the white sleeves and pink sash and cap.

The very first time this livery had hit the winner's circle had been with a horse called Charming Native at Windsor on May 14, 1979 and it turns out that the sash and cap should have been orange. 'Before I started as an owner,' says Prince Khalid, eyeing the green and orange-clad room in Paris on Thursday, 'Lord Weinstock came to see me in my office and looked around at the curtains and wallpaper and said, "You have your colours here." Someone misunderstood the instructions, but after Windsor I thought it would be unlucky to change.'

After Known Fact the ambition began to take on another dimension. While other big winners, notably Dancing Brave, the greatest of them all, still came from the yearling sales, the idea of forming a breeding operation was taking shape. 'When I was at the sales,' says Prince Khalid, 'I realised that it would be easier to buy horses and race them, but I got the feeling that this was not enough, that it would be more fun to do what people like the Aga Khan and Lord Howard de Walden did and build up your own families.'

So it was that the Juddmonte empire began. Studs were bought in England, Ireland and America; Known Fact became the sire of champion miler Warning; Arc winner Rainbow Quest fathered the first Juddmonte Derby winner Quest For Fame in 1990; and Dancing Brave the second when Commander In Chief stormed clear at Epsom in 1993. The previous year Juddmonte had nine worldwide Group 1s, but the following year proved to be an *annus mirabilis*, with Zafonic, a product of their American operation, taking the 2,000 Guineas as part of a season that saw top strikes in Britain, France, Ireland and America.

Interviewing Prince Khalid for the *Sunday Times* before the Derby that year was to note the exactness of the detail gathered by Philip Mitchell, then, as now, general manager of the prince's five European studs – three in England and two in Ireland.

As this year with Bullet Train and Workforce, in 1993 Juddmonte were two-handed in the Derby with Commander In Chief being less fancied than Tenby, who started favourite. And, as this year, Abdulla was not into overelaboration.

'I rely on very good professionals,' he had said in his London study with a huge canvas of some 16th century Italian battle hanging above his desk. 'I just hope we can get some of it right.'

The current total of 156 Group 1 victories, 125 of them with home-breds, is testimony to that hope fulfilled, as is the success of Dansili and Oasis Dream as outstanding young stallions in Europe, and Belmont winner Empire Maker in America. But 17 years on from that first conversation, and after another 18 Group race wins in another golden year of 2003, there were a few more clues as to just how much the man who is listed on racecards as plain Khalid Abdulla cares about his operation.

The first evidence is from those who work for him: from Dr John Chandler and Garrett O'Rourke in America, to Rory Mahon in Ireland, and Mitchell and racing manager Teddy Grimthorpe in England. Talk to any of them and they will tell you not of a noisy hands-on employer, but of a quiet man who, in the words of Grimthorpe, 'likes things to be done properly'.

On Thursday, Prince Khalid was happy to explain. 'It is still my only hobby,' he says with a degree of self-mocking sadness, 'but while I have very good people working for me, I like to be involved.

'We have budgets on everything because you cannot say to managers that you should just go and spend, that's not good for anyone. When I first said to Lord Weinstock that I was going to have horses I did not expect to make money, and we are not really doing that, but it is all within reason. At one stage I felt the operation was getting too big. It is important for me to be able to deal with one manager.'

To that end, Grimthorpe (who took over from Grant Pritchard-Gordon in 1998) is briefed by the trainers of the 250 horses spread almost evenly between England and France and with some 40 in America, and reports every evening to his patron wherever he may be in the world. By the time he does so, the miracle of satellites means he will be talking about a race that the prince has already watched.

The search, of course, is for excellence, not mere indulgence, and the key to Abdulla's interest is in his fascination as to how his equine families are working out. 'I have my stud book with me all the time,' he says. 'With breeding, I think the dam is the key more than the stallion. With a bad dam, nothing is going to work out. We have to sell to keep the standard. With unraced mares [such as Workforce's dam Soviet Moon] it is a judgement. I cannot take any credit for Workforce but at least we did not sell the dam.'

What he can take credit for is the way he can get others to pursue excellence on his behalf. Not just on mating lists, on which he gives approval; or on allocation of horses to trainers, which is entirely his own responsibility; but in quality control, instantly obtained and present from the very beginning of a horse's life. Within minutes of an enquiry to Mitchell about Workforce's development, a series of documents come across by email detailing everything from the moment of birth – 9.44pm at the Side Hill Stud on March 14, 2007, to his emergence 'as a genuine Derby contender'.

If you must know, the only documented query on Workforce's first night was that the newborn foal did not suck on his mother's milk until 3.20am, but by the time he got to Ireland in November that year his birth weight of 62kg had grown to a hefty 356kg and Mitchell's otherwise complimentary comments contain the proviso 'could get too big'.

A year later, when Workforce had already grown to 16 hands and 525kg, that caveat must still have seemed a danger and it says much for the team's judgement and facilities that he could be kept back to take his time and complete his early exercise with Joe Mahon at Ferrans Stud in Ireland. In fact Workforce did not arrive at Sir Michael Stoute's until June 6, 2009 and the feat that he achieved in being able to run and win brilliantly at Goodwood on September 23 that year says as much for his early preparation as it does for his own talent and that of his trainer.

But that is only one story of a pupil in the scholarship stream. This week Abdulla has an 18-strong roster of star home-breds coming up for highly prized, highly public examinations.

Starting with Deluxe, half-sister to Dansili and Banks Hill, taking on the Aga Khan stars Sarafina and Rosanara in this afternoon's Prix de Diane, before Ascot week beckons with major challenges at every turn. [Deluxe finished fourth behind Sarafina in the Prix de Diane.]

Whatever happens to the brilliant but exasperating Zacinto in the Queen Anne on Tuesday, more will be expected of Twice Over and Byword, joint-favourites for the Prince of Wales's on Wednesday, from Showcasing, high in the lists for the Golden Jubilee at the end of the week and even more from Manifest, hot favourite for the Gold Cup – which is just about the only major race that an Abdulla horse has never won. [Zacinto was fourth behind Goldikova in the Queen Anne, Byword and Twice Over filled the first two places in the Prince of Wales's, Showcasing was a disappointing last of 24 in the Golden Jubilee, while Manifest finished tenth to Rite Of Passage in the Gold Cup.]

This is about as exciting as Flat racing gets, and your first impression of the impassive features on the rather slight, but immaculately dressed, figure at the centre of the Juddmonte team might make you think he was not experiencing it. 'But I do enjoy it,' insists Abdulla as we closed, 'I like being in England, like visiting my horses and going to the races. But I don't like showing myself and talking to the press. I don't think it suits me really.'

Courteous as ever he takes me to the door and an aide hands me an umbrella for the soft drizzle outside.

The nearby Parc Monceau is exactly a kilometre in circumference and on Thursday was peopled by sweaty runners on their lunch-hour jog. The place is famous as the site, on October 22, 1797, of the first parachute jump when a man called Andre-Jacques Garnerin floated unsteadily to earth after cutting himself free from a hotair balloon at 3,000 feet. British and French, and indeed all racing fans, might be excused for thinking that 54 years ago something equally wondrous dropped down from above.

The trainer:
Sir Henry Cecil

On the eve of Royal Ascot 2012 **Alastair Down** *visited Warren Place to interview Sir Henry Cecil about his extraordinary life and the extraordinary horse who had put the icing on the cake of his career – a career which began in 1969 and has included ten trainers' championships, 25 British Classics and 75 winners at Royal Ascot.*

Newmarket doesn't do hills, just the one really – Warren by name. And at the top of it stands a single training establishment, Warren Place, home and place of work for Sir Henry Cecil, by popular acclaim the racing public's favourite trainer.

And when things are going well and the Group-race winners are rattling home along railway lines, being on top

Henry Cecil with Frankel and Shane Fetherstonhaugh after a gallop, June 2012

of the hill is the right and proper place to be, and time was when Cecil was lord of all he surveyed. Warren Place was indeed a bed of roses, in more ways than one.

And then out of a seemingly cloudless sky, aided and abetted by illness and personal tragedy, it all went horribly askew. Cecil's wasn't a fall from grace but it was a vertiginous plummet from pre-eminence. Suddenly a racing superpower shrank to a tinpot third-world state and between July 2000 and October 2006 a yard that used to hammer home big-race wins like rivets could not muster a single Group 1.

Cecil says: 'Life is about highs and lows and my lows lasted six or seven years. I went from 200 horses to little over 30 and none of them was ever going to take me to Ascot.

'Out on the Heath there were trainers saying, "That's Henry Cecil over there – should have retired years ago".'

And there were plenty who thought that Henry had somehow boarded a train bound, if not for oblivion, then for the outer peripheries of insignificance. But beneath Cecil's dandified exterior is a foreign legionary's toughness and a fighting cock's instinct for survival. When, in that trademark physical gesture, he hangs his head to one side you have to remember that his neck sits atop a spine of steel.

He appears to have reached an armed truce with his cancer, some sort of hard-fought equilibrium. But the death in 2000 of his twin brother David is a hurt that can never be truly healed. The old adage 'there is no secret so close as that between a rider and his horse' would be true only if the world held no twins. When the heart of one beats, the other's thuds on the off-beat and when one dies the surviving half can never be completely whole again.

Cecil recalls: 'It was at about my lowest point that Jane came into my life and I could never overstate what she has done. And of course I have children and they all needed me not to be a pathetic wreck.

'It got so bad that I was dragging myself out of bed in the morning. I was never not working, but the horses I was training were hardly inspirational. My PR skills were useless and, frankly, I didn't really want to be seen.

'When things are going well year after year you take things for granted. You get complacent and expect another good season by right, then suddenly you take a look and find you are 178th on the trainers' list.

'I am not clever and anyone will tell you I have no common sense, but I have always had a certain amount of pride.'

And did he realise during those stagnant days adrift in the doldrums that beyond the walls of Warren Place there was a racing public aching for him to be back in the big time? He pauses for thought and says: 'The public's reaction when I started to be successful again was very moving and it still is. They have always been so fantastic to me and I really don't know why.'

As a rule, the public can get a look round Warren Place and its famous garden when Cecil stages his annual opening day in aid of charity but this year, with all the buzz surrounding Frankel, an invasion of around 3,000 people would have raised complex security issues. Cecil's garden is very special, although he pooh-poohs the popular notion that he is some guru of the rose-growing world.

'I buy roses and appreciate them but that doesn't make me an expert,' he says – just as someone who enjoys a plate of the finest roast beef is not an authority on cattle. But he is rightly proud of Warren Place's immaculate surroundings which contain some genuine rarities, including the famous Mummy's Peas which are descended from peas discovered in the tomb of Tutankhamen and a Wollemi pine, one of the world's oldest and rarest varieties of tree only discovered in 1994.

How Cecil managed to get his horticultural hands on a Wollemi pine is slightly mysterious but, somewhere along the line, it appears to involve a certain 'Alan Titmarsh' – as when Cecil mentions the gardener and broadcaster the 'ch' is notable for being silent. You can contrast that silence with the roar that will greet Frankel at Ascot on Tuesday if he can send the royal meeting stratospheric by winning the opening Queen Anne Stakes.

Ever since Frankel stormed home on his seasonal return in the Lockinge, Cecil has not been short of advice on his horse's future programme which, according to some, should range from the July Cup to the Breeders' Cup taking in every trip along the way plus igniting the flame at the Olympic opening ceremony.

Cecil is too sage to sigh but he chooses his words with care and says: 'Frankel is quite a complicated person and I have got to know him very well. With this horse it has always been about doing what is best for him and I have peace of mind about the way he has been trained.

'He used to pull very hard – always trying to do too much – and it has taken a long time to get him to relax. Early on in his career we had never had a young horse who took so much out of himself but was still able to finish his races.

'In his pedigree, while you have Sadler's Wells up top, there is a lot of fast blood down below. The fast blood is the weaker blood, but it is still fast.

'I am looking forward to running him over a mile and a quarter, but I don't want to do it at Eclipse time and that is one of the reasons we will go to York. I know it is an extra half-furlong, but Sandown is a much stiffer track.'

And then Henry, slightly exasperated and as if to scratch a slightly annoying itch, adds: 'People keep banging on and asking why we run him in races against inferior opposition?

'There are several answers including the fact that any race you run a horse in you want to win. And you would be mad to say you were not going to run in a particular Group 1 race because it is too easy. And it is not my fault – or Frankel's – that other horses are inferior.

'I would say that Camelot is a good horse although it is possible that the opposition among three-year-old colts is not particularly strong. Wouldn't it be lovely to see Frankel and Camelot race against each other, although it looks as if Camelot's programme has already been worked out, doesn't it?'

And looking back, was there a particular moment when, to Cecil's long-practised eye, Frankel suddenly soared? He replies: 'I suppose the first time he confirmed in public that he could be anything was in the Royal Lodge at Ascot – it was the way he went round the outside and took them on the bend. The others were completely dead by the time they came round the corner and he won by ten lengths. It was significant for no other reason than we have all seen a lot of morning glories.'

It was after that performance that Channel 4's Jim McGrath, one of the outstanding judges of his generation, walked off the stands with the simple comment: 'That is the best two-year-old I have ever seen.' And now Henry has his favourite stamping ground in his sights – the royal meeting.

He says: 'I am looking forward to next week, but Ascot is not an easy course. It could be that Frankel will prove better over a mile and a quarter. He does most of his work over about seven and a half furlongs but I might work him over further – say nine furlongs – just to convince myself, although I have watched him so bloody much I really ought to know by now!

'He does his work with Bullet Train, but he isn't competition – he is just a lead horse so occasionally I drop another one in as well.

'Looking further ahead, we now have British Champions Day and we have to build on that – we need to support it. There is talk of the Breeders' Cup, but do I really want to race him on dirt? I have two priorities, the horse and Prince Khalid, and their best interests are the same.'

Depending how Frankel fares in his owner's Juddmonte International at York, Cecil will have the choice of another Queen Elizabeth II Stakes or the Champion Stakes itself at Ascot in October.

Watching Frankel you are convinced he would have the speed to win a July Cup, but Cecil has spent endless hours teaching the horse to burn his fuse slowly, so why suddenly give him a hair trigger again simply for the sake of showing off for a little over a minute?

Frankel is all about power and with power comes responsibility. How, after Frankel's unforgettable blitz in the 2,000 Guineas, he was ever made amenable to restraint again is both a mystery and a testament to Cecil's ability to get inside a horse's head. And it is abundantly clear that a strong bond has developed between Cecil and Khalid Abdulla, whose loyalty to his trainer never wavered through those years when the wolves howled at the gate of Warren Place.

Henry says: 'The prince has been a very good friend to me and helped me on so many occasions – it was he who sent me off to the Mayo Clinic in America when I was ill.

'He is quiet and generous-spirited, but he doesn't suffer fools, so goodness only knows why he suffers me. I think everyone knows that I adore Twice Over, who is now in his sixth season here. He has made me appreciate how dreadful it must be for jumps people when something happens to a horse they have had for years – it must be heartbreaking.

'I get the feeling that the prince may have received a good offer for Twice Over during the winter, but he knew there would be a tear in my eye if I saw him leave and one day he rang Teddy Grimthorpe and told him that Twice Over would stay in training. That says a great deal about the man.

'And of course I get attached to horses. Old Ajaan has been here forever and although he is only a handicapper he has become special – he is a Niarchos horse and Maria Niarchos is someone who has been incredibly loyal to me.

'But Juddmonte has been a lovely organisation to work for and that comes from the top. As long as the prince has horses I will go on training and continue to do my best for him. But if for some unforeseeable reason he ever stopped owning horses, I don't think I would want to be training any more.'

Cecil and I end our meeting with a tour of the garden, partly because he wants to show it off in the best sense of the word but also because, outdoors, he can sneak a cigarette. At 69 and having passed through a fire or two, the ludicrous glamour of his youth now has a bit of mileage on it, but like some vintage Bentley Continental he remains a thing of impeccable style.

Henry loves quality above everything – be it in horses, clothes, gardens or people. Many years ago, when he set new records, seemed invincible and carried the world of the Flat before him, his success seemed almost effortless, although nothing of that order of magnitude is ever built without a deal of graft underpinning the genius.

And of course Warren Place is his fiefdom from where his flag flew after those innumerable Group 1s.

Then for a grim count of seasons it all went to ashes and the house on the hill must have become his prison. Nothing is more remarkable about this complex, flawed and fabulously talented horseman than that he nailed the lie inherent in that horrible old cynic's adage 'They never come back.' And if you can't warm to his triumph second time round there is something wrong with you.

The jockey:
Tom Queally

Brough Scott *profiles Tom Queally, the man who rode Frankel in all his 14 races.*

Moonshadow was a full-sister to the Oaks winner Love Divine. She was beautifully bred but desperately slow. She may yet earn fame as a dam of Classic winners but she has already left one small mark on the racing story. At Lingfield on November 9, 2006 she was the first horse that Tom Queally rode for Henry Cecil. However, Frankel she most definitely was not.

It was Moonshadow's seventh and final attempt to prove herself a racehorse and she duly finished a fading sixth of 12 and had her targets changed from the parade ring to

Tom Queally celebrates after Frankel's victory in the 2012 Juddmonte International Stakes at York

the breeding paddocks. Yet for the then just 22-year-old Tom Queally it had been an opportunity to die for. 'I was really thrilled,' he said, 'and although I could not get hold of Henry on the telephone, when I saw him in the street at Newmarket to say "Thank you" he asked me to ride work for him the next season. He's a genius to work for.'

In 2007 most of the Cecil connection was on the gallops but Queally did ride one winner, Lady Lil at Pontefract, for Warren Place from 14 rides, and 2008's 18 winners from 90 rides blossomed into a full-blown 215-ride 2009 stint and a 41-winner scorecard which included the Nassau Stakes at Goodwood, the Champion Stakes at Newmarket, not to mention the small matter of Midday's ground-breaking win in the Breeders' Cup Filly and Mare Turf in California.

There was also the 'sinned-against' short-head defeat in the 2009 Oaks, matched by the photo-finish victory but 'deemed-the-sinner' demotion in the 2010 1,000 Guineas. It has not been an uneventful union. 'Sometimes,' says Tom Queally in that quiet, thoughtful way of his, 'I can't believe I am only 27.'

For while it was the Cecil link, and a dramatic opening Group 1 victory on the 'spare ride' Art Connnoisseur for Michael Bell in Ascot's 2009 Golden Jubilee which catapulted Queally into the big time and over £2 million in UK prize-money that year, it was way back at Clonmel in April 2000 that the winning had begun. Everyone was impressed as this 15-year-old schoolboy and former southern area pony racing champion drove an hitherto unsuccessful four-year-old called Larifaari between horses to land the first of what are now over 700 winners on the Queally card. It was to prove an almost too explosive start.

For if in that opening season the boy was initially just keen to do anything trainer Pat Flynn said en route to landing the Irish Apprentice Championships, the parents were insistent that schooling at The Christian Brothers in Dungarvan must come first. By February 2001 Declan Queally had unsuccessfully applied to the Turf Club to have his son's indentures transferred to his own small yard in Waterford and by October it had become a very public dispute finally resolved by the Turf Club ruling that the Flynn/Queally contract should be terminated a year early as 'relationships between the parties had irretrievably broken down'.

Tom does not want to revisit the issue except to say how much he now appreciates his parents insisting on his finishing his education to the extent of getting Leaving Certificate (Irish equivalent of A-Levels) grades better than many fellow pupils not encumbered by another life on the track. 'My mum would pick me up at 12 o'clock,' he says, 'and I would study my school work as well as form on the way to the races and be back in school next morning.'

After the split with Pat Flynn, weekends would be spent riding out with Aidan O'Brien to whom Tom went full-time in 2003. But while the Ballydoyle experience was invaluable and even provided a shock first Group winner when the pacemaker Balestrini slipped the field in the Ballysax Stakes, it did not fuel a winner increase or a change in the perception that the young man from Cappagh somehow thought too much of himself. At the end of 2003, with a score of just 11 on the board, Queally told O'Brien that he needed to try his luck overseas.

'Aidan was very good about it,' says Tom with the self-possession some have taken as conceit or even idleness, 'and if I had ridden three more winners that year I would probably still be in Ireland. Hand on my heart I was not cocky, but when you are an early success and handle yourself with a degree of confidence the papers can take against you. I felt sorry for my mum and dad and knew I should try somewhere different.'

The road to the Cecil saddle was not a direct one. In January 2003 Queally had spent several weeks with David Elsworth at Whitsbury and ridden the winner of a 'seller' at Lingfield. The next winter he had a spell work riding at The Fair Grounds in New Orleans and then travelled down to New Zealand where he rode a winner and so impressed experienced owner Doug Rawnsley that he was then and there predicting an international future. 'He possessed brains, good manners, beautiful hands, flair and balance,' Doug wrote to me, 'It was obvious that he had great potential but he told me that he had nothing lined up and was about to accept a job as a work-rider in Lambourn.'

A father figure was needed and, as it has for a string of jockeys including Jamie Spencer and Frankie Dettori, it appeared in the slow-talking, hard-smoking, cryptic but benign shape of Barney Curley. He may be a stewards' challenge and a bookmakers' nightmare. And over the years Barney may have cost Tom a 21-day suspension for 'not making sufficient effort' on the oddball Zabeel Palace in 2007 and involved both Tom and his younger Limerick University student brother Declan in a bookie-busting coup in April 2010, but when it comes to caring for young men's futures no one doubts Barney's credentials. He does not just play the father figure, he gives them a sense of perspective.

'In the winter of 2008,' Queally explains, 'Barney said to me 'you have a big season up ahead and I am now going to take you to Zambia to make sure you realise how lucky you are'. What I saw down there with the work he's doing with DAFA [Direct Aid For Africa] stops you ever feeling sorry for yourself if you are in a traffic jam after riding three beaten favourites at Sandown.'

Queally was speaking in the summer of 2010 in what was the seventh season since he had arrived in Newmarket and promptly won the apprentices' title in Britain with 66 winners in 2004, although he did not top the 100-mark until five years later. The coolness which would become such a feature of his Frankel partnership was presaged by the phlegmatic calm with which he handled the Oaks and 1,000 Guineas enquiries with Midday and Jacqueline Quest. 'If you are going to try and kick the stewards' room door down,' he said, 'you are not going to get the race back but you do make yourself look an idiot. And it's a privilege for me to be riding for Henry when you consider he has had the likes of Pat Eddery, Steve Cauthen and Lester Piggott.'

'Henry is fantastic to ride for,' Tom continued. 'I understand what he wants from me and I think he understands what I can do for him. He has this way with his horses, is so at one with them. It is as if he has something extra. I could stand here and talk about him for an hour and not do him justice.' Through all the mounting hyperbole of the Frankel journey Queally has continued with a stance of such self-effacing respect for his employer that he is rarely drawn into discussing Frankel except during the after-race euphoria of one of their many triumphs.

But he made a revealing exception one hot, cheery but far from superstar evening at Epsom in July of Frankel's third and final season. 'Yes it's ordinary racing,' he said sitting on a wooden bench outside the weighing room, 'yet I am racing every day of the season and only on six days of it will I be on Frankel. He may pay a lot of the bills but you have to keep a grasp on reality. At the end of the day, I am doing a job and whatever calibre of horse comes along there is a job to be done. Frankel may be different but he is not that different. He is still a horse and I would like to think that I do him justice by treating him the same as any other horse. If you let the occasion, or the enormity of the task you take on board get to you, or you treat it any different, that's when it becomes different. If you treat it the way you would any other horse, or any other task you undertake, I think that's the way to get the maximum out of it.'

'The key to Frankel is that he has a will to win like no other horse I have ever sat on. He just pours it on at the two-furlong marker. He quickens and lengthens in five strides like one of those boxers who hit you with a combination and it's all over. The biggest problem I usually have is pulling him up. As I came back at Ascot [after the Queen Anne Stakes] it was quite frightening to think that something so good could actually get better. He used to be quite fiery but he has grown up so much. If he was a person he would be like one of those real laid-back guys to whom you still would not want to say the wrong thing. He is very sensible now and is a very nice horse to have anything to deal with.'

'Yes it's a job,' he had said in that week before a second Sussex Stakes wonderclass at Goodwood, 'but I admit Frankel is different. He's fantastic and it would be a lie to say that Wednesday is the same as any other race. Yet you have to try.' But then in almost muscle-memory reaction against hyperbole, Tom Queally curled his lip and said, 'Look, I just ride the horse. I am not going to get carried away and make a film star of myself. I would rather slip quietly out the back door of the weighing room and go home.'

So on 14 consecutive occasions he has returned to scenes of mounting adulation as Frankel has galloped his way into immortality. The centre of that applause has always been the horse and master trainer Henry Cecil not the young man from Cappagh on his back. The jockey has liked it that way.

The inspiration:
Bobby Frankel

Two days before Frankel astonished the racing world with a lung-busting display in the 2011 Qipco 2,000 Guineas the Post *published an article by* **Julian Muscat** *about Bobby Frankel, the late trainer who did so much for Juddmonte that they named their brightest star after him.*

It is not just the horse who generates reverence. Mention the man after whom Frankel is named and anyone connected with Juddmonte Farms will let out a deep sigh.

Bobby Frankel, who succumbed to cancer at the age of 68 17 months ago, was a man with two sides. To those beyond his circle of friends he could be brash beyond belief. To those on the inside he was a constant source of inspiration. His daughter Bethenny found fame in *The Real Housewives of New York City*, the American reality series, but Frankel – opinionated, plain-speaking and possessed of a sharp wit – was very much the stereotype from Brooklyn. His veins coursed with New York blood even though he lived his last 37 years in California.

How he came to train for Juddmonte is the stuff of fantasy. In the mid-1980s, when Khalid Abdulla's managers saw opportunity in the rich turf programme out on the west coast, they crunched the numbers in their quest for the right trainer. Frankel's name kept coming to the fore despite his relatively low profile and he was duly chosen.

His appointment to the prestigious position raised many eyebrows. To him were entrusted horses who fell just short of the highest class in Europe. He would take them on the remainder of a journey that added considerable lustre to Juddmonte's burgeoning stud book.

Frankel made his reputation by claiming horses and improving them, often beyond all recognition. However, his alliance with Juddmonte swept him straight into the major league. He won five Eclipse Awards as America's leading trainer, the last four of them in consecutive years from 2000. He trained the winners of 3,654 races for prize-money earnings of $228 million. No wonder the numbers stacked up.

American trainer Bobby Frankel,
after whom the wonder horse
was named

There's an uncomfortable parallel between Frankel and the man who trains his equine namesake. Frankel was overtaken by cancer, which Henry Cecil continues to wrestle with. Abdulla was as moved by Frankel's fight as he is by Cecil's ongoing battle. For the prince, there must be succour in the symmetry that one of his two adopted sons revives memories of the other through the conduit of a magnificent racehorse.

That horse was a standout at Juddmonte from the day he was foaled. It takes plenty for one thoroughbred's physical qualities to elevate him beyond the herd of regally bred contemporaries in the Juddmonte paddocks, but Frankel was that horse. The pick of the foal crop remained the pick of the yearling crop, which is rare in itself. And the ignominious history of yearling sales-toppers underlines how rare it is for the pick of any yearling crop to match expectations on the racecourse. In Frankel's case, the sense of providence is unavoidable.

Mind you, Frankel is not the first Juddmonte homebred to provoke great expectations. In 2001 a yearling colt by Unbridled so captivated staff at Juddmonte's American annexe that they obtained odds of 100-1 against him winning the Kentucky Derby two years down the line. The colt in question was Empire Maker, whose preparation for the race was compromised by a bruised foot, yet he still ran a mighty race for Frankel to chase home Funny Cide.

Funny Cide duly won the Preakness to set up a Triple Crown tilt, but Frankel was piqued at the attention accorded

Funny Cide. 'All this pre-race bull don't mean a thing,' he growled the day before the Belmont. 'We'll see who's the better horse.' Empire Maker duly obliged, prompting Frankel to exclaim: 'Redemption – I learnt a new word today.' Empire Maker is sire of Cecil's Derby hope World Domination.

Appropriately, the last big winner Frankel trained was Juddmonte's Champs Elysees in the Grade 1 Canadian International at Woodbine in October 2009. He'd previously excelled with Champs Elysees' siblings, winning Grade 1 races with each of Heat Haze, Cacique and Intercontinental, the last-named winner of the 2005 Breeders' Cup Filly & Mare Turf from the mighty Ouija Board.

For Juddmonte's broodmare band, Frankel made equine luminaries of Ryafan, Ventura, Wandesta and Sightseek, who won seven Grade 1 races in an exemplary career. However, his own roots were nothing like so aristocratic. The son of parents with a kosher catering business, he lasted one day at college after a brawl and committed himself to assiduous form study for betting purposes.

He was 21 when he took $40 to the races and returned home with $20,000. 'I put the money on my mother's bed,' he reflected years later. 'She thought I had robbed a bank.'

From there, he worked at the track in the mornings, walking horses that had just been exercised in exchange for a free pass to the races in the afternoons. He took out a training licence in 1966 and caused a sensation from the moment he transferred to California in 1972.

During the spring meeting he sent out a record 60 winners at a strike-rate of 33 per cent. Yet all the while he wrestled with a conscience that couldn't countenance anything but the best for any animal; he missed the Breeders' Cup in 2007 because one of his dogs was ill.

Frankel's link with Juddmonte allowed him to distance himself from the murky world of claiming horses. He was not sorry to leave it all behind him. He was among the first to eschew the common practice of racing horses hard, preferring instead to target races with fresh horses. His hackles were raised by a journalist as he prepared Native Guest for the 1975 Preakness Stakes. Told that his colt, who had run just four times, might lack seasoning, Frankel replied: 'Really? Well, remind me to add some salt and pepper to his hay.'

Those who worked in Frankel's orbit speak as one of his profoundly emotional attachment to his horses. Some years after he had somehow patched up the fragile Exbourne – who had chased home Nashwan in the 1989 2,000 Guineas – to win big races in the US, he came across Exbourne's headstone at Juddmonte Farms in Kentucky. In an instant he broke down uncontrollably.

It would have moved Frankel deeply to know that Abdulla – whose horses he trained to the bitter end, having dispersed the rest of his string – had named a colt in his memory. And if he is looking down on Saturday, victory for the powerful bay would surely reduce him to floods of tears.

'Bobby was a huge part of Juddmonte's success for 20 years,' says Abdulla's racing manager, Teddy Grimthorpe. 'He was an exceptional horseman, but more than that, he was a very special person.'

*Ghostzapper wins the Breeders'
Cup Classic at Lone Star Park in
2004 for Bobby Frankel*

Beginnings

Breeding Frankel

Nancy Sexton *examines the genetic cocktail which produced the best racehorse in the world.*

As the likely measure by which greatness in the racehorse will be judged in years to come, it is fitting that Frankel's background is a blend of influences stemming from three of the most powerful breeding operations of the past century.

Frankel is not one of those rags-to-riches horses who defied his breeding. He is a son of Coolmore's four-time champion stallion and 2001 Derby winner Galileo, whose record of 30 Group 1 winners at the relatively young age of 14 places him within the great sires of all time. Such has been his ascent that it will be surprising if he doesn't one day surpass the achievements of his own sire, the 14-time champion Sadler's Wells.

And his dam, Kind, hails from a family that was cultivated by the leading American owner John 'Jock' Hay Whitney before passing into the hands of Frankel's breeder Prince Khalid Abdulla, for whom it is currently thriving. Frankel was bred to be good and he is a rare example of the volatile elements of racehorse breeding coming together to yield superlative results.

When Kind was sent to Galileo in early 2007, he had already been represented by the Classic winners Nightime and Sixties Icon and champion two-year-old Teofilo from just two crops of racing age.

In turn, she was a talented daughter of another Coolmore colossus in Danehill and a half-sister to Powerscourt, a Group 1-winning son of Sadler's Wells.

Since then, we have come to regard the Galileo – Danehill cross as one of the most potent of recent years. Such is Galileo's dominance that he crosses well with most lines, particularly Roberto and Shirley Heights. But nothing can touch the Galileo – Danehill nick, the combination behind six Group 1 winners including Teofilo, Maybe and Golden Lilac in addition to Frankel.

Today, the Juddmonte operation is vast, encompassing farms in Europe and Kentucky that include two stallion bases which in 2012 housed nine stallions. Bar the odd yearling purchase, the fleet of approximately 500 horses in training are homebreds.

Kind at Banstead Manor Stud in September 2012

Frankel boasts three generations of Juddmonte breeding but even so in another year he could have been running for John Magnier, Michael Tabor and Derrick Smith as the product of an arrangement with Coolmore whereby Juddmonte would annually send ten mares to Sadler's Wells and then to his sons, Galileo and Montjeu. One operation would have first pick one year and the other operation have first pick the following year.

It was an arrangement that benefitted both parties as for Juddmonte it produced Soviet Moon, the dam of Workforce, while for Coolmore it yielded Brian Boru, Powerscourt and Await The Dawn.

Luckily for Juddmonte, they had the good fortune to have first pick in 2008, the year that Kind delivered Frankel.

Trained by Roger Charlton, Kind was a totally different animal to her celebrated half-brother. Powerscourt excelled over 1m2f to 1m4f but his year-younger sibling was a free-going sort who owned plenty of speed, an attribute often associated with progeny of Danehill.

She was held in some regard from the outset, running third as the 6-4 favourite on her debut over 6f on Kempton's old turf track. Although turned over at short odds on her next two starts, she went on to rattle up a five-time winning sequence over 6-7 furlongs culminating in victory in the Listed Flower of Scotland Stakes at Hamilton.

As a four-year-old, she added the Listed Kilvington Stakes at Nottingham as well as a third in the Group 3 Ballyogan Stakes, and retired as the winner of six of 13 starts and £72,402.

Kind's early days included several fiery moments – she unshipped Richard Hughes twice before breaking her maiden at Kempton – and there was a suspicion that had she been easier to settle, she probably would have been effective over a mile as well. Charlton was quoted as saying after she won her second race that he believed she wasn't a 'natural sprinter' but nevertheless she was armed with a high cruising speed and progressed with racing to develop into a formidable opponent in her own grade.

Juddmonte sent Kind to Sadler's Wells himself in her first year at stud and the resulting foal was Bullet Train, the Lingfield Derby Trial winner who later fulfilled pacemaking duties for Frankel.

The fact that Bullet Train stayed 1m4f suggested that the distance could be within reach of Frankel – after all, he is by a Derby winner who is an influence for stamina. But while Frankel possessed too much speed to be given the option of tackling 1m4f, the indicators from his pedigree are borne out by the performances of his younger brother Noble Mission.

A later-developing type than Frankel, Noble Mission's day in the sun came in 2012 when he collared subsequent St Leger hero Encke on the line in the Gordon Stakes at Goodwood to become his dam's third Pattern winner from as many foals. His profile suggests there will be more to come as a four-year-old.

Few mares are capable of producing one Pattern winner let alone three in as many years so at the age of 11, Kind already deserves to be mentioned in the same breath as some of the breed-shaping mares of the past.

That is something which not only pays tribute to the breeding methods of Juddmonte but to John 'Jock' Hay Whitney, a former US ambassador to the United Kingdom whose stable was a leading force in America for over 40 years until the early 1980s, as well as to the foresight of Prince Khalid Abdulla's first trainer Jeremy Tree.

Tree was entrusted with Abdulla's first horses in training and duly sent out his first winner, Charming Native, and first Classic winner, the 1980 2,000 Guineas winner Known Fact.

The acquisition of top-notch broodmares and fillies, primarily through agent James Delahooke, for the fledgling operation followed and it is many of those early shrewd purchases who today provide the backbone to Juddmonte.

A pivotal moment in the expansion was Abdulla's 1983 purchase of a private package of mares from the dispersal of Jock Whitney, a transaction in which Tree played an influential role. Not only did the package include Frankel's fourth dam, the Stage Door Johnny mare Rockfest, but also Peace, dam of Whitney's 1976 Coronation Cup winner Quiet Fling and the ancestress of Abdulla's Group 1 winners Byword, Proviso and Zambezi Sun.

Whitney, the American ambassador to the United Kingdom in the late 1950s and early 1960s, hailed from a family steeped in American racing history and he himself bred 132 stakes winners including champions Capot and Tom Fool. However, he derived much pleasure from racing in Europe and for many years sent horses to Beckhampton to be trained by Jeremy Tree. It was an interest that maintained a family tradition ignited at the turn of the 20th century by his grandfather William Collins Whitney, who leased the 1901 Derby winner Volodyovski. Another family member, uncle Harry Payne Whitney, raced the 1913 2,000 Guineas third Whisk Broom.

Nine horses bred under the Beckhampton banner by Jock Whitney recorded stakes success including Quiet Fling but one of his greatest contributions was as the breeder of the iconic hurdler Sea Pigeon.

European influences are also evident in the background of Whitney's Belmont Stakes winner Stage Door Johnny, a son of Prince John who was out of a Ballymoss daughter of a French-bred mare. Stage Door Johnny, a strapping blaze-faced chestnut who stood at Whitney's Greentree Stud in Kentucky, developed into a prominent broodmare sire and left a lasting impression on the Juddmonte-Whitney package as the sire of Rockfest and Peace's Listed-winning daughter Intermission, the dam of 1987 1,000 Guineas third Interval and Grade 2 winner Interim.

Whitney's involvement with Rockfest's family spanned only nine years, starting when Tree paid 15,000gns for her dam, Rock Garden, as a yearling. The daughter of Roan Rocket was bred by Lady Wyfold but like many of Wyfold's stock, was sold as a foal, in her case for 4,600gns.

Rock Garden boasted a fine family that for many years was the mainstay of Wyfold's Sarsden House Stud in Oxfordshire. Her dam, Nasira (by Persian Gulf), was a minor winner over a mile and out of Circassia, a sister to Wyfold's high-class two-year-old Rustam and half-sister to the 1951 1,000 Guineas winner Zabara, whom Wyfold bred and sold to Sir Malcolm Alpine. In turn, they were out of Baron Wyfold's 1942 Queen Mary Stakes heroine Samovar.

Today, Circassia features as the ancestress of Group 1 winners Don't Forget Me, Desert King (whose granddam Loose Cover established a world mark for a mile at Brighton) and Maroof in addition to Frankel. Another branch descending from Samovar yielded the brilliant Mtoto and 1984 Oaks heroine Circus Plume.

Rock Garden won a mile Chepstow maiden as a three-year-old for Tree and Whitney and spent the early part of her stud career in Britain before travelling to America, where her third visit to Stage Door Johnny resulted in Rockfest, her only black-type performer from ten foals. Rockfest won two races for the Tree-Whitney alliance although her best performance came when second in the 1982 Lingfield Oaks Trial. As a four-year-old, she passed into the hands of Juddmonte, for whom she produced 13 foals led by Rainbow Lake, her 1990 daughter of Rainbow Quest.

As could be expected of a filly by stamina influence Rainbow Quest out of a daughter of the late-maturing Stage Door Johnny, Rainbow Lake benefitted from the more patient approach. Trained by Sir Henry Cecil, she raced solely as a three-year-old, winning her second race, a 1m4f Haydock maiden, in a canter before taking the Listed Ballymacoll Stud Stakes at Newbury. Connections opted to bypass the Oaks and instead headed to the Lancashire version, in which she trounced Talented by seven lengths despite meeting trouble in running.

Such was the ease of her victory that she was sent off favourite against older fillies of the calibre of User Friendly, for her next assignment, the Yorkshire Oaks, but she found little under Pat Eddery and finished nearly 17 lengths adrift of the winner Only Royale. Her career finale, the Park Hill Stakes, was similarly disappointing and she was subsequently retired with her early promise seemingly unfulfilled.

Even without the exploits of Kind, Rainbow Lake could be regarded as a highly successful broodmare. Seven of her 15 foals have won, headed by Powerscourt, who was saddled by Aidan O'Brien to win the Tattersalls Gold Cup and Arlington Million before retiring to Coolmore's Ashford Stud in Kentucky. He sired the 2009 Moyglare Stud Stakes winner Termagant in his first crop but was sold in early 2010 to stand at the Turkish Jockey Club.

Another son, the Rail Link colt Last Train, ran a narrow second in the 2012 Grand Prix de Paris.

As for Kind, she has a two-year-old Oasis Dream colt, Morpheus, who was unplaced on his first start for Sir Henry Cecil. She also has a yearling filly by Oasis Dream and at the time of writing is back in foal to Galileo.

The efforts of three leading breeders of their time – Baron and Lady Wyfold, Jock Whitney and Khalid Abdulla – have combined over 100 years to cultivate a female family of capable of producing horse of the calibre of Frankel. The question now is whether Frankel can develop into the top sire that is hoped of him.

What is for certain is that he won't be short of opportunity. There is no sire line currently more powerful in Europe, if not the world, than Sadler's Wells, and for 11 seasons, Coolmore were able to offer breeders two leading sons in Galileo and Montjeu until the latter's death in 2012.

Galileo has, for some time, laid claim to being the best sire in the world. An attractive physical specimen who boasts a brilliant pedigree (out of Arc heroine Urban Sea and a half-brother to Sea The Stars) and champion race record to match, he is the sire of 69 Group winners – and counting – including 30 at Group or Grade 1 level. Remarkably, 11 of those 30 won at the top level during 2011 alone.

He has also wasted no time in emerging as a powerful sire of sires. At the time of writing, there are four sons of Galileo at stud with runners and two – New Approach and Teofilo (bred on the same Danehill cross as Frankel) – have sired Dewhurst Stakes winners out of their first crops. The other two, Heliostatic and Sixties Icon, have also sired stakes winners despite not arguably receiving the best opportunities.

So not only will Frankel attract the interest of top international breeders when he moves back to Banstead Manor Stud but he will also be well supported by Juddmonte, an operation which owns one of the best broodmare bands in the world and is backed up by a tightly knit team in the best position to utilise him to good effect.

All being well, Frankel's first two-year-olds will hit the track in 2016. It will be fascinating to see how he fares.

Frankel: bay colt, born February 11, 2008

		Nearctic	Nearco
			Lady Angela
	Northern Dancer		Native Dancer
Sadler's Wells		**Natalma**	Almahmoud
		Bold Reason	Hail To Reason
			Lalun
	Fairy Bridge		Forli
		Special	Thong
Galileo (b 1998)		Mr Prospector	Raise A Native
			Gold Digger
	Miswaki		**Buckpasser**
		Hopespringseternal	Rose Bower
Urban Sea		Lombard	Agio
			Promised Lady
	Allegretta		Espresso
		Anatevka	Almyra
		Northern Dancer	**Nearctic**
			Natalma
	Danzig	Pas De Nom	Admirals Voyage
			Petitioner
Danehill		His Majesty	Ribot
			Flower Bowl
	Razyana	Spring Adieu	**Buckpasser**
			Natalma
Kind (b 2001)		Blushing Groom	Red God
			Runaway Bride
	Rainbow Quest	I Will Follow	Herbager
			Where You Lead
Rainbow Lake		Stage Door Johnny	Prince John
			Peroxide Blonde
	Rockfest	Rock Garden	Roan Rocket
			Nasira

Bred by Juddmonte Farms in Britain
Horses in bold type have multiple appearances in the pedigree

Frankel's pedigree

SIRE: GALILEO

Bred by D. Tsui and Orpendale in Ireland. Won 6 of 8 starts (1m – 1m4f) at 2–3 years inc. 1 out of 1 at 2 years, five out of 7 at 3 years inc. Derby (Gr1), Irish Derby (Gr1), King George (Gr1) and Derrinstown Stud Derby Trial (Gr3). Also second Irish Champion Stakes (Gr1). RPR 113 at 2 and 132 at 3. Champion 3yo in Europe in 2001. Earned £1,621,110.

By a 14-time champion stallion who is now a leading sire of sires and damsire. Out of champion Urban Sea, the 1993 Arc winner and a half-sister to 2,000 Guineas winner King's Best. A half-brother to seven winners inc. Urban Ocean (c Bering; Listed winner, sire), Melikah (f Lammtarra; Listed winner and Classic-placed, dam of Masterstroke [Gr2]), Black Sam Bellamy (c Sadler's Wells; Group 1 winner, sire), All Too Beautiful (f Sadler's Wells; Group 3 winner and Classic-placed, dam of Wonder Of Wonders [Classic-placed]), My Typhoon (f Giant's Causeway; Grade 1 winner), Sea The Stars (c Cape Cross; champion and Classic winner, sire) and Born To Sea (c Invincible Spirit; Listed winner and Classic-placed). Outstanding

family formerly cultivated by Gestut Schlenderhan in Germany.

Retired to stud in 2002. Stands at Coolmore Stud, Co. Tipperary at a private fee. From eight crops of racing age sire of G1 winners Alandi, Allegretto, Cape Blanco, Cima De Triomphe, Frankel, Galikova, Golden Lilac, Great Heavens, Igugu, Imperial Monarch, Lily Of The Valley, Lush Lashes, Mahbooba, Maybe, Misty For Me, Nathaniel, New Approach, Nightime, Niwot, Red Rocks, Rip Van Winkle, Roderic O'Connor, Sans Frontieres, Sixties Icon, Soldier Of Fortune, Sousa, Teofilo, Together, Treasure Beach and Was.

Champion sire in Britain and Ireland in 2008, 2010, 2011 and 2012.

DAM: KIND

Bred by Juddmonte Farms in Britain. Won 6 of 13 starts (5-7f) at 3-4 years inc. 0 out 2 at 2 years, 4 out of 6 at 3 years inc.

Listed Flower of Scotland Stakes and 1 out of 5, Listed Kilvington Stakes, at 4 years. Also third Ballyogan Stakes (Gr3). RPR 70 at 2, 91 at 3 and 108 at 4. Earned £72,402.

Well-bred. By a top sprinter who became a champion sire in both hemispheres, a leading sire of sires and damsire. A half-sister to dual (1m2f-1m3f) Group 1 winner Powerscourt (by Sadler's Wells) and out of Rainbow Lake, the seven-length winner of the 1993 Lancashire Oaks. Further

family of 1951 1,000 Guineas winner Zabara and champion sire Rustam.

To stud at 5 years and dam of: Bullet Train (2007 c Sadler's Wells; Group 3 winner), Frankel (2008 c Galileo; unbeaten champion and multiple Group 1 winner), Noble Mission (2009 c Galileo; Group 3 winner), Morpheus (2010 c Oasis Dream).

She also has a yearling filly by Oasis Dream and is in foal to Galileo.

Frankel the infant

A few days after Frankel had blazed away from his rivals to win the Juddmonte International Stakes at York in August 2012, **Julian Muscat** *looked back to the colt's earliest days.*

Aidan O'Brien stood at a discreet distance, some way removed from the throng surrounding Frankel, his eyes misty at what he had seen. In the winner's circle stood the colt who had just blown away St Nicholas Abbey in the Juddmonte International.

As he admired the horse it was impossible to tell whether O'Brien was aware that he might easily have welcomed the young Frankel into his Ballydoyle stables three years ago. In which case the story surrounding the horse many describe as the best they have seen would have been very different indeed.

When Frankel was a foal Juddmonte and Coolmore had entered into an arrangement where Juddmonte supplied some mares to be covered by Coolmore stallions. Every year, when all the foals were born, one party would take first pick, then the other, and so on until all the foals were allocated. It was Juddmonte's good fortune to have first pick in the year Frankel was foaled.

Who knows what would have happened had it been Coolmore's turn to pick first? Perhaps O'Brien was reflecting on that very subject. By all accounts Frankel was an attractive foal, which would not have been lost on Coolmore's team of talent-spotters. But his physical appearance alone may not have determined his prominence on their wishlist.

In the circumstances, with a selection of beautifully-bred foals to choose from, Coolmore might have set greater store on a filly whose bloodlines they coveted. Breeding is a long-term game: Coolmore may have had one eye on the future and their desire to breed from her long after her racing career had ended.

Nevertheless, the process of choosing those foals must have resembled a game of high-stakes poker. The process of alternate picks happens every day in school playgrounds, yet in this version of it those making the choice had scant evidence with which to work.

Frankel as a foal

And Coolmore had done well from their previous picks. They included dual Group 1 winner Powerscourt, out of Frankel's granddam Rainbow Lake; and in the same year St Leger winner Brian Boru out of Eva Luna – from whom Coolmore also got Kitty O'Shea, a winner twice from as many starts before she suffered a career-ending injury when favourite for the Oaks in 2005.

On this occasion the Juddmonte team had ample time to size up the foal born in box 5 at Banstead Manor Stud's foaling unit, on the fringe of Newmarket, in the evening of February 11, 2008. Weeks later, the foal and his mother, Rainbow Lake's daughter Kind, were sent back to Coolmore for a repeat tryst with Galileo.

Frankel thus spent three months grazing at Coolmore, where he will have been keenly observed by the staff. Whatever their aspirations, he left for good when he returned to Banstead Manor with Kind in May. From that day his progress was such that he was always among the cream of Juddmonte's 170-strong foal crop.

Staff at the farm remember him for the fact they had very little to do with him. He rarely came to their attention. He was never ill, nor did he sustain any injury that required treatment. In that respect he was happily anonymous.

His medical record was as clean as his limbs, which were noted by stud manager Simon Mockridge on the day Frankel was born. "Quality colt, tall with size and scope. Strong hind legs. Very good foal," Mockridge recorded. He weighed in at a healthy 123lb.

Stud groom Jim Power's early thoughts on Frankel are recorded on Juddmonte Farm's website. "He was a straightforward yet sensitive horse with a slight air of arrogance about him," Power relates. "He never gave you any problems but he was very inquisitive and attentive to what was going on around him. He was always the first one to come up to you and was the type of foal who would defy you not to take notice of him."

His weaning from Kind was uneventful until, in September 2008, he was shipped to New Abbey Stud in Ireland. While there he was given a rating of 7++ by stud manager Rory Mahon.

All Juddmonte's foals are graded on a scale of one to ten by the outfit's key personnel. This often leads to discrepancies, since beauty is in the eye of the beholder, but Frankel won universal acclaim. He was admired by all who assessed him.

It is rare for any Juddmonte foal to earn a mark of eight. Nor are foals graded on their commercial appeal. The grading is strict, taking into account minor blemishes in conformation and general demeanour. All foals are assessed on a monthly basis prior to an end-of-year report.

With a 7++ to his name, Frankel already stood out. Yet as anyone who has graded horses will affirm, those who win the pageant rarely emerge as the best racing talent. That's the beauty of racing: there is no telling what lurks inside the body and soul of any thoroughbred, irrespective of his physical appearance.

Mahon's records show that Frankel stood on good limbs and that his temperament was equable. His effervescence would only become manifest when he entered training with Sir Henry Cecil in Newmarket.

From New Abbey, Frankel transferred to nearby Ferrans Stud, where he was broken in as a yearling in September 2009. Even then he remained calm; there was no observation from Mahon that he required a good rider, which is Mahon-speak for a headstrong youngster. "Good temperament, rides well, nice colt," is how he assessed Frankel. It wasn't long before Frankel showed glimpses of his raw potential when trotting and cantering at Ferrans.

Simultaneously, over at Banstead Manor, Juddmonte's personnel were pondering names for the yearlings who were soon to embark on their racing careers. They were also lamenting the death of their principal American trainer. Bobby Frankel succumbed to cancer in November 2009, leaving a gaping emotional hole along with memories of his flair in honing numerous champions for Juddmonte.

Juddmonte's proprietor, Khalid Abdulla, duly resolved to name a horse after him. The horse would have to befit the name, and so it was bestowed upon the bay colt who was by now seen as Juddmonte's most promising young talent.

The new year's dawn saw Frankel continue to impress at Ferrans, where he was now trotting and cantering over a mile each day. Two weeks later and his level of fitness was deemed sufficient for Juddmonte staff to inform Cecil his arrival was imminent.

On January 14, 2010, Frankel stepped off the horsebox to begin life at Warren Place. The rest, as they say…

Following spread: *Frankel makes a winning debut from Nathaniel on a wet Newmarket July Course*

Frankel the two-year-old, 2010

6.35 RACE 3

European Breeders' Fund Maiden Stakes (Class 4)
Winner £4,533.20

RUK

1m July

£7,000 guaranteed **For** 2yo, which are E.B.F. eligible **Weights** colts and geldings 9st 3lb; fillies 8st 12lb
Entries 31 pay £35 **Penalty value 1st** £4,533.20 **2nd** £1,348.90 **3rd** £674.10 **4th** £336.70
YB £10k Racing Post Yearling Bonus Scheme qualifier   ADJUSTED AVERAGE WINNING RPR 97

1 (11)
BRETON STAR YB
b c Medicean-Wannabe Grand
D M Simcock J M Cook
2 9-3
Chris Catlin

2 (1)
CASTLEMORRIS KING
br c And Beyond-Brookshield Baby
M C Chapman C O'Connell
2 9-3
Robert L Butler(3)

3 (3)
COLOUR VISION (FR) YB
gr c Rainbow Quest-Give Me Five
M Johnston Sheikh Hamdan Bin Mohammed Al Maktoum
2 9-3
Adrian Nicholls

4 (4)
225 **DORTMUND** YB 48 **BF**
b c Dubawi-Zacheta
Mahmood Al Zarooni Godolphin
2 9-3
Antioco Murgia(7)
92

5 (12)
ELRASHEED
b c Red Ransom-Ayun
J L Dunlop Hamdan Al Maktoum
2 9-3
Richard Hills

6 (10)
FRANKEL
b c Galileo-Kind
H R A Cecil K Abdulla
2 9-3
Tom Queally

7 (2)
GENIUS BEAST (USA)
b c Kingmambo-Shawanda
Mahmood Al Zarooni Godolphin
2 9-3
Ahmed Ajtebi

8 (7)
6 **LEMON DROP RED** (USA) 21
b c Lemon Drop Kid-Skipper's Mate
E A L Dunlop R J Arculli
2 9-3
Tom McLaughlin
65

9 (5)
37 **MAHER** (USA) 29 **BF**
b c Medaglia d'Oro-Bourbon Blues
D M Simcock Sultan Ali
2 9-3
Kieren Fallon
86

10 (6)
MAN OF GOD (IRE) YB
b c Sadler's Wells-Jude
J H M Gosden B E Nielsen
2 9-3
Saleem Golam

11 (8)
NATHANIEL (IRE)
b c Galileo-Magnificient Style
J H M Gosden Lady Rothschild
2 9-3
William Buick

12 (9)
6 **BONITA STAR** YB 15
b f Beat Hollow-Catch
M R Channon B P York
2 8-12
Alan Munro
91

2009 (8 ran) **Dashing Doc** (6) D R C Elsworth 2 9-3 11/4F   Philip Robinson RPR78

BETTING FORECAST: 7-4 Frankel, 7-2 Nathaniel, 11-2 Elrasheed, Genius Beast, 13-2 Dortmund, 12 Maher, 16 Colour Vision, Man Of God, 25 Bonita Star, 33 Breton Star, Lemon Drop Red, 66 Castlemorris King.

European Breeders' Fund Maiden Stakes

Newmarket, August 13, 2010

It was in early July 2010 that Frankel received his first mention in the Racing Post *– a full six weeks before his eagerly anticipated debut – when Steve Dennis visited Warren Place to see Sir Henry Cecil as part of a series of articles that the paper devoted to the legendary trainer.*

Dennis wrote about the talent in the stable in that summer: 'And there is a host of well-bred two-year-olds waiting in the wings for their cue, including… a Galileo half-brother to Bullet Train called Frankel.'

Cecil is renowned for being patient with his juveniles, and he told Dennis that his owners, in particular the Niarchos family and Prince Khalid Abdulla, never put him under any pressure to race them. One of Cecil's many strengths is his ability to feel his way with racehorses and knowing when and where to run them.

Cecil's promising juvenile had plenty to live up to, and even at this early stage Frankel was already putting in some eyecatching work on the Newmarket gallops, including with his year-older three-parts brother Bullet Train, who won the Lingfield Derby Trial that spring.

Frankel, who held entries for the Dewhurst Stakes, Racing Post Trophy and the following year's Investec Derby, was unleashed in public for the first time in the European Breeders' Fund Maiden Stakes over a mile on Newmarket's July Course.

Among his opposition that summer evening were the unraced pair, Nathaniel and Colour Vision, but it was Frankel who made an immediate impression, as **Peter Scargill** *reported:*

Khalid Abdulla and Bobby Frankel enjoyed many successful days together as owner and trainer until the latter's death last year, and the prince may have found a way to pay fitting tribute to the legendary handler with a win by the horse named in his honour.

Frankel, trained by the equally legendary Henry Cecil, oozed quality as he landed the 1m juvenile maiden on his debut under Tom Queally.

The 7-4 favourite, a three-parts brother to Lingfield Derby Trial winner Bullet Train, quickened well in the rain-soaked ground to score by half a length from Nathaniel.

Cecil said: 'He's done it well on that ground and could be a nice horse if he goes the right way. He's in the Royal Lodge and the Racing Post Trophy, but we'll have to see how he is. He'll stay at a mile for now.'

Sandeep Gauravaram leads Frankel into the winner's enclosure

5049	EUROPEAN BREEDERS' FUND MAIDEN STKS	1m
	6:35 (6:36) (Class 4) 2-Y-O	£4,533 (£1,348; £674; £336) **Stalls** Low

Form					RPR
	1		**Frankel** 2-9-3 [0] .... TomQueally 10		93+
			(H R A Cecil) *gd sort: w'like: scope: dwlt: hld up: hdwy over 2f out: led ins fnl f: shkn up and r.o: readily*	**7/4**[1]	
	2	½	**Nathaniel (IRE)** 2-9-3 [0].. WilliamBuick 8		92+
			(J H M Gosden) *w'like: scope: tall: chsd ldr tl led over 2f out: rdn over 1f out: hdd ins fnl f: r.o*	**3/1**[2]	
	3	5	**Genius Beast (USA)** 2-9-3 [0] .... AhmedAjtebi 2		81
			(Mahmood Al Zarooni) *w'like: scope: lw: chsd ldrs: outpcd over 2f out: styd on to go 3rd wl ins fnl f*	**15/2**[3]	
225	**4**	hd	**Dortmund**[48] [3449] 2-8-10 [83]................................ AntiocoMurgia[7] 4		81
			(Mahmood Al Zarooni) *led over 5f: sn rdn: no ex fnl f*	**15/2**[3]	
6	**5**	1 ¾	**Bonita Star**[15] [4508] 2-8-12 [0] .... AlanMunro 9		72
			(M R Channon) *prom: rdn over 1f out: hung lft and wknd ins fnl f*	**20/1**	
30	**6**	5	**Maher (USA)**[29] [4054] 2-9-3 [0] .... KierenFallon 5		66
			(D M Simcock) *trckd ldrs: racd keenly: edgd lft and wknd over 1f out*	**8/1**	
	7	½	**Elrasheed** 2-9-3 [0].. RichardHills 12		65
			(J L Dunlop) *lengthy: hld up: hdwy over 2f out: sn wknd*	**25/1**	
	8	½	**Man Of God (IRE)** 2-9-3 [0] .... SaleemGolam 6		64
			(J H M Gosden) *str: scope: bit bkwd: hld up: hdwy over 2f out: wknd over 1f out*	**16/1**	
6	**9**	shd	**Lemon Drop Red (USA)**[21] [4318] 2-9-3 [0] .... TomMcLaughlin 7		64
			(E A L Dunlop) *chsd ldrs: rdn over 2f out: hung lft and wknd over 1f out*	**33/1**	
	10	14	**Castlemorris King** 2-8-10 [0]................................... AdamBeschizza[7] 1		33
			(M C Chapman) *w'like: cl cpld: s.s: sn prom: wknd over 2f out*	**100/1**	
	11	1 ¾	**Colour Vision (FR)** 2-9-3 [0] .... AdrianNicholls 3		29
			(M Johnston) *leggy: s.s: sn pushed along and rn green in rr: lost tch over 2f out*	**25/1**	
	12	3 ½	**Breton Star** 2-9-3 [0]... ChrisCatlin 11		21
			(D M Simcock) *leggy: s.s: a in rr: wknd over 2f out*	**66/1**	

1m 43.69s (3.69) **Going Correction** +0.50s/f (Yiel)   **12** Ran   SP% 119.8
Speed ratings (Par 96): **101,100,95,95,93 88,88,87,87,73 71,68**
toteswingers:1&2 £2.30, 2&3 £3.90, 1&3 £3.50   CSF £6.30 TOTE £3.10: £1.60, £1.70, £2.70;
EX 7.80.
Owner K Abdulla **Bred** Juddmonte Farms Ltd **Trained** Newmarket, Suffolk

Analysis

GRAHAM DENCH

Frankel's home reputation preceded him to the track and he started a warm favourite for a maiden with a strong tradition.

Held up towards the outside in a race contested by well-bred individuals from many top stables, he made his ground smoothly from three out and, having challenged between horses, came clear with Nathaniel in the final furlong.

While not so spectacular as subsequent Derby winner Motivator in the same race in 2004, it was a highly encouraging debut and he was always comfortably on top in the closing stages. What we had no way of knowing at the time was that this would turn out maiden form of the very highest order.

Nathaniel raced only once more at two but went on to beat Derby winner Workforce in the following year's King George VI and Queen Elizabeth Stakes and Farhh in the 2012 Eclipse. Way back in eleventh place in this Newmarket maiden was the 2012 Ascot Gold Cup winner Colour Vision.

4.25
RACE 6

Frank Whittle Partnership
Conditions Stakes (Class 2)
Winner £10,904.25

ATR

7f

£17,500 guaranteed **For** 2yo which have not won a Class 1 or 2 race **Weights** colts and geldings 8st 12lb; fillies 8st 7lb **Penalties** for each Class 5 race won 2lb; for each Class 4 race won 4lb; for each Class 3 race won 6lb (nursery handicaps excluded for the purpose of penalties) (penalties cumulative and maximum penalty 12lb) **Allowances** horses which have never run 3lb **Entries** 23 pay £85 **Penalty value 1st** £10,904.25 **2nd** £3,265.50 **3rd** £1,632.75 **4th** £817.25 **5th** £407.75 ADJUSTED AVERAGE WINNING RPR 102

1 (3)	**1**	**FARHH** 48 **D**1 b c Pivotal-Gonbarda Saeed Bin Suroor Godolphin	2 9-2 Frankie Dettori 104
2 (4)	**1**	**FRANKEL** 28 b c Galileo-Kind H R A Cecil K Abdulla	2 9-2 Tom Queally 107
3 (5)	9256127	**COLORADO GOLD** 26 ch c Dubawi-Yanka P F I Cole Goldswain,Jefferson,McLaughlan,Williams	2 9-0 Silvestre de Sousa 99
4 (1)	4248126	**DIAMOND GEEZAH** (IRE) 22 **D**1 b c Diamond Green-Lanark Belle B W Hills Rebel Racing	2 9-0 Michael Hills 105
5 (2)		**RAINBOW SPRINGS** b f Selkirk-Pearl Dance J H M Gosden George Strawbridge	2 8-4 Nicky Mackay

2009 (3 ran) **Al Zir** (3) Saeed Bin Suroor 2 9-2 30/100F   Frankie Dettori RPR107

BETTING FORECAST: 11-10 Frankel, 13-8 Farhh, 7 Diamond Geezah, 10 Rainbow Springs, 20 Colorado Gold.

Frank Whittle Partnership Conditions Stakes

Doncaster, September 10, 2010

Frankel, who received quotes of 25-1 for the Derby after his debut, had his second start on the third day of Doncaster's St Leger festival. The form of his debut success had been boosted the previous day when his stablemate Picture Editor beat Nathaniel a short head.

Cecil said before the race: 'Frankel is very well and seems to have come on for his first race. We are happy with him.'

The race was set to be no formality, though, as among the four-strong field was Godolphin's Farhh, a six-length

Frankel's longest winning margin – 13 lengths

winner on his debut on Newmarket in July. As was reported in the Post *the following day, Frankel moved up a gear on Town Moor:*

Frankel looked a colt of huge potential in the 7f conditions contest. Despite pulling hard under Tom Queally, the pair strode clear of their two remaining rivals – Farhh had been withdrawn at the start and Colorado Gold was a non-runner – for an impressive 13-length victory.

Cecil said: 'It's a shame the other horse [Farhh] was withdrawn because we'd have learnt a bit more. It was promising, he couldn't have done any more.

'It's been a long time since I had a two-year-old as promising as him. He's in the Royal Lodge and Racing Post Trophy but not the Dewhurst, we will just feel our way and see how he is and what the prince wants to do. He could be very special but he's not there yet.'

THE RESULT

Analysis

GRAHAM DENCH

Frankel was left with a simple task in this St Leger week conditions race following the withdrawal of Godolphin's Farhh, who became worked up in the stalls. Even allowing for that, this was a spectacular performance.

Having allowed Michael Hills on Diamond Geezah to give Frankel a lead for five furlongs or so, Tom Queally let out a little rein around two furlongs out and the race was soon as good as over. He looked utterly different class as he sprinted away in blistering style to win by the widest-margin of his career, yet just weeks later 13-length runner-up Rainbow Springs finished an excellent third in the Group 1 fillies' race at Longchamp on Arc day.

2.30 RACE 2

Juddmonte Royal Lodge Stakes BBC2
(Group 2) (Colts & Geldings) (Class 1)
Winner £70,962.50   1m Rnd

£125,000 guaranteed **For** 2yo colts and geldings **Weights** 8st 12lb **Penalties** a winner of a Group 1 or Group 2 race 3lb **Entries** 126 pay £370 **1st Forfeit** 42 pay £400 **Confirmed** 10 pay £290 **Penalty value 1st** £70,962.50 **2nd** £26,900 **3rd** £13,462.50 **4th** £6,712.50 **5th** £3,362.50 **6th** £1,687.50

1 (5)   218 **ESKIMO** (IRE) [98]   t2 8-12
b c Galileo-Dietrich   Ryan Moore
A P O'Brien (IRE)   Mrs John Magnier, M Tabor & D Smith   (98)

2 (2)   11 **FRANKEL** [15 D1]   2 8-12
b c Galileo-Kind   Tom Queally
H R A Cecil   K Abdulla   (130)

3 (1)   41 **HAPPY TODAY** (USA) [26 D1]   2 8-12
b c Gone West-Shy Lady   Richard Hughes
B J Meehan   Jaber Abdullah   (99)

4 (3)   11531 **KLAMMER** [35 BF]   2 8-12
b c Exceed And Excel-Aymara   Kieren Fallon
Jane Chapple-Hyam   Yan Wah Wu   (118)

5 (6)   56124 **SLIM SHADEY** [16 C1]   2 8-12
br c Val Royal-Vino Veritas   Liam Keniry
J S Moore   Phil Cunningham   (112)

6 (4)   2112 **TREASURE BEACH** [12 BF]   2 8-12
b c Galileo-Honorine   J Murtagh
A P O'Brien (IRE)   D Smith, Mrs J Magnier, M Tabor   (114)

2009 (10 ran) **Joshua Tree** (5) A P O'Brien 2 8-12 12/1   C O'Donoghue RPR111

BETTING FORECAST: 30-100 Frankel, 7 Treasure Beach, 16 Klammer, 20 Happy Today, Slim Shadey, 25 Eskimo.

Juddmonte Royal Lodge Stakes

Ascot, September 25, 2010

The welcome revival in Cecil's fortunes in the previous few years had occurred without conspicuous success in the two-year-old division – his last Group 1-winning juvenile was Passage Of Time in 2006 and the last two-year-old colt he had trained to win a Group 1 was King's Theatre in 1993.

On Frankel's prospects of staying the Derby trip, for which he was now as short as 8-1 favourite, Cecil added: 'He's a half-brother to Bullet Train, who doesn't really get a mile and a half, but Frankel is by Galileo, so he may stay, although their dam was a sprinter.'

Prince Khalid's racing manager Teddy Grimthorpe said five days before the Royal Lodge: 'He had a nice time at Doncaster and has thrived since. With his looks and pedigree we have to be excited. He has enormous potential, but it's one step at a time and we are not going to crown him a champion before he has even run in a Group race.'

As well as being favourite for the Derby, Frankel was disputing favouritism for the 2,000 Guineas with Pathfork and Saamidd in what was quickly developing into an exciting crop of two-year-olds.

Since its inception in 1986 the Racing Post *has developed its own ratings system whereby its experts rate the performance of every horse after every race.*

Racing Post Ratings' Simon Turner identified Frankel's 2,000 Guineas potential when he gave him a figure of 114, which was a noteworthy mark on just his second start, for his Doncaster victory in a performance where he showed abundant speed over 7f.

The hype was building, and 'Frankel Fever' was one headline on the front page of the Post *on the day of the Royal Lodge Stakes at Ascot, noting how Henry Cecil had stated that Frankel 'could be very special' after the Doncaster race.*

Grimthorpe added: 'We think he is a pretty exciting prospect and those credentials are on the line. I don't think the ground will be a great issue. They're calling it good now and are expecting a bit more rain, but that won't be a huge worry. He could go either for the Dewhurst or the Racing Post Trophy after this. He'll have the option of one or the other.'

Under the headline 'FRANKEL'S AWESOME – Cecil hails his best juvenile in 40 years after "monster" colt wows Ascot', **Lee Mottershead** *reported a sensational Ascot victory:*

What we saw with our own eyes was thrilling enough. When, a few moments later, we heard the words of Henry Cecil, the excitement, buzz and anticipation was only heightened. Few and far between are performances that truly take the breath away, but in romping to an exhilarating ten-length success in Ascot's Juddmonte Royal Lodge Stakes, the already magnificent Frankel delivered such a display.

Unbeaten in his previous two starts, Frankel – named by race sponsor and owner Khalid Abdulla after the late, great US trainer Bobby Frankel – entered the Ascot stalls as favourite for both the 2,000 Guineas and the Investec Derby. And after exhibiting both explosive speed and rare brilliance to secure this Group 2, he is between 2-1 and 5-2 for the Newmarket Classic and as short as 5-2 for Epsom.

Anyone contemplating a Derby wager must consider Cecil's strong feeling that Frankel's stamina could be insufficient for the 1m4f test. Anyone just happy to soak up the splendour of a stunning thoroughbred can reflect on Cecil's remark that not since Wollow, the champion two-year-old of 1975 and subsequent Guineas winner, has he trained a better juvenile.

Cecil was not alone in being dazzled. Jockey Tom Queally described the son of Galileo as a monster, while Aidan O'Brien, whose Treasure Beach and Eskimo finished third and fourth, opted for the word unbelievable.

The manner of Frankel's success certainly veered towards that adjective. Initially settled at the back of the five-runner field, Frankel was allowed an inch of rein at the beginning of the home bend. Within a handful of strides, the 30-100 favourite had passed every one of his rivals in a rapid rush that evoked memories of Arazi's Breeders' Cup-winning move. Once in front, he stayed there, with the smart Klammer winning the secondary race behind him.

Frankel at full stretch during his Royal Lodge Stakes romp

'He was very impressive,' admitted Cecil. 'He has been ticking all the right boxes and in the last two months has started to really improve. I think he has a lot of talent and, given the way he works, I don't think I've had a better two-year-old since Wollow, and that's nearly 40 years ago.

'He's just a baby and I think there's improvement in him. He has plenty of scope and isn't just a two-year-old. I think he's above-average and has a bit of potential. He's exciting.'

Assessing Frankel's future, Cecil added: 'I'd question whether he'll get the Derby trip. The dam was very fast and his dam side has come out in him. He has a lot of class and could easily be a Guineas horse. Now we have to decide between the Dewhurst and the Racing Post Trophy. It depends entirely how he does from now to Newmarket, but I'd rather finish him a bit earlier.'

Queally added: 'As I edged him out he got a bit carried away and went from second gear into fifth. That's three

AIDAN O'BRIEN
champion trainer

If his trainer is saying that is the best two-year-old he has had for nearly 40 years, it's very hard to argue with that man. It was unbelievable.

JIMMY LINDLEY
former jockey and BBC pundit

I've been a fan since the first time he raced. If he'd got beaten today, I'd have packed up and gone home. He has balance and stature, and I think he's an exceptional horse. I would be very surprised if he gets beaten if he runs again this season, and if I were a betting man – which I'm not – I'd back him to win both the Guineas and the Derby.

JIM MCGRATH
Channel 4 pundit

He's one of the best two-year-olds I've ever seen. He looked extraordinary at Doncaster, and today, on different ground, he has confirmed that impression. People say he hasn't yet beaten a top-class horse – and as yet he hasn't – but he gives the impression that when he has to, he will.

races now and he's never had a smack. I don't know yet whether he has it all, but he appears to have a lot of it.'

Klammer's partner Kieren Fallon said his mount had been 'no match for the winner'. And quite how good that winner could be, nobody knows. Not even his trainer.

'We'll keep our fingers crossed, but I think he's slightly out of the ordinary,' said Cecil.

His will not be the only fingers crossed.

Alastair Down *was as bowled over by Frankel's Ascot performance as everyone else who witnessed it.*

Within a minute of Frankel passing the post yesterday the slightly aggravating 'ding-dong' that signals a stewards' inquiry sounded out across Ascot – presumably because they wished to ask Henry Cecil why he had run a three-year-old in the Royal Lodge.

It is tempting to say that victories such as this are the lifeblood of the game, but few have ever seen a victory like this. Arguably the sagest and most clinically minded judge in racing walked off the stand seconds after Frankel had won and delivered himself of the opinion: 'That could be the best two-year-old I have ever seen.'

Henry Cecil didn't seem inclined to disagree with this view. Though clearly trying to keep his suede loafers on the ground, the sheer spine-realigning excitement of Frankel's win kept breaking through. He said: 'I haven't had a better two-year-old since Wollow' and those of you still young enough to go clubbing should understand Wollow ruled the juvenile roost back in 1975, so his trainer was telling us that in 35 years of Newmarket mornings he had not seen anything to compare with Frankel.

When Frankel won last time out at Doncaster he may have beaten only trees and loiterers, but he did so in a time that had the clockers thinking of sending their stopwatches in for an overhaul. But this was a performance, in a Group 2, from another stratosphere and, on a card that boasted a brace of Group 1s and a Frankie four-timer, Frankel towered over the afternoon like Gulliver in Lilliput.

Cecil said: 'In the last two months all he's done is improve, improve and improve.' Even someone with maths as bad as mine makes that three 'improves', and you can take it from Henry there is hardly a pigeon left unplucked on Warren Hill.

Henry Cecil after the Royal Lodge Stakes as the photographers train their lenses on Frankel

Henry was in ripping form, and the great thing about him is that he goes off on the most endearing tangents as he debriefs the press. Thus we learned 'I don't believe in ante-post' when told Frankel was 2-1 favourite for the Guineas, and he poured cold water on the idea of his colt getting the Derby trip because of the dominance likely to be exerted by his dam's side, which is laden with speed.

'Females are the stronger sex, you see,' opined Henry, and who are we to disagree with the great man?

If he had told us he prefers mashed potatoes to roast with his partridge I wouldn't have been surprised and, having given long thought as to why this high patrician strikes such a chord with the ordinary racing fan, it is that he doesn't hide anything. He tells it as he sees it, and you can see his feelings etched in his face.

It was interesting that one of the first things Cecil picked up on was that Frankel had settled well in a race that was run at a bit of an early dawdle. Tom Qieally also highlighted how amenable the colt had been with the memorable description: 'He can take a bit of a bite early on.' Oh to have the everyday Irishman's way with words.

Queally added: 'He's got a buzz to him that is deadly at the end of a race. I wasn't shocked by the way he won because I see him in the mornings. He's so good that he just leaves them behind.'

But what Frankel left behind was the promise of what may be to come. There will be no need for Henry Cecil to jet off anywhere hot this winter, he can just bask in the warmth of the afterglow left by this performance.

Pointing out that Frankel has plenty of scope, Cecil made an early entry for the Understatement of the Decade award when observing that Frankel was 'above average' before rightly upgrading him to 'very exciting'.

It will be interesting how highly Frankel is rated by the analysts and anoraks. This may not have been a Royal Lodge with any real depth to it, but the way he went whoosh when Queally asked him to go round his field between the four and three pole looked the stuff of which racing magic is made.

It would be an exaggeration to say that the Ascot authority thought of abandoning the rest of the card for lack of interest, but neither the thrilling nose victory of Poet's Voice nor Dettori's splendid echo of his definitive Ascot day were a patch on Frankel.

And the fact that he may well not have the genetic wherewithal for a mile and half may be a blessing. A Derby preparation is an incredibly difficult exercise because the early stage at which it comes in the season means you are always trying to force a quart into a pint pot on the time front – plus the fact that Epsom can't half haul some horses about.

Notwithstanding the still mildly inexplicable victory of Harbinger, this was the most indelible triumph of the season and a two-year-old performance of the highest conceivable rank. Now we can look forward not only to a potential champion but a Henry Cecil champion, and a 2011 season built round that mouthwatering prospect could be golden indeed.

6347	**JUDDMONTE ROYAL LODGE STKS (GROUP 2) (C&G)**	**1m (R)**
	2:30 (2:31) (Class 1) 2-Y-O £70,962 (£26,900; £13,462; £6,712; £3,362)	**Stalls** High

Form					RPR
11	**1**		**Frankel**[15] 5912 2-8-12 0.. TomQueally 2		123+

(H R A Cecil) *lw: scope: gd sort: t.k.h: hld up in last: swtchd lft and gd hdwy on bit to ld ent fnl 3f: shkn up and readily qcknd clr over 2f out: wl clr and nudged along after: v impressive* **30/100**[1]

| 1532 | **2** | 10 | **Klammer**[35] 5323 2-8-12 99... KierenFallon 3 | | 101 |

(Jane Chapple-Hyam) *lw: t.k.h: trckd ldrs: rdn and outpcd by wnr over 2f out: chsd clr wnr and hung rt u.p over 1f out: kpt on but no ch w wnr* **11/1**[3]

| | **3** | ³/₄ | **Treasure Beach**[12] 6043 2-8-12 0.................................... JMurtagh 4 | | 101 |

(A P O'Brien, Ire) *w'like: leggy: t.k.h: trckd ldrs: rdn and n.m.r wl over 2f out: sn rdn and nt pce of wnr: pressing for modest 2nd whn hmpd and swtchd lft over 1f out: kpt on same pce after* **11/2**[2]

| 0 | **4** | 1¼ | **Eskimo (IRE)**[98] 3190 2-8-12 0....................................(t) RyanMoore 5 | | 97 |

(A P O'Brien, Ire) *swtg: led and set stdy gallop: hdd and rdn ent fnl 3f: nt pce of wnr and btn 2f out: lost 2nd and squeezed against rail over 1f out: wl btn and styd on same pce after* **20/1**

| 6124 | **5** | 2¾ | **Slim Shadey**[16] 5880 2-8-12 101...................................... LiamKeniry 6 | | 91 |

(J S Moore) *pressed ldr tl rdn and dropped to rr wl over 2f out: outpcd and wl btn ent fnl 2f* **16/1**

1m 41.73s (1.03) **Going Correction** +0.40s/f (Good)   5 Ran SP% 111.3
Speed ratings (Par 107): **110,100,99,98,95**
 CSF £4.80 TOTE £1.30: £1.10, £3.20; EX 4.10 Trifecta £1197.40 Pool: £67,159.76 - 41.50 winning units..
Owner K Abdulla **Bred** Juddmonte Farms Ltd **Trained** Newmarket, Suffolk
■ Stewards' Enquiry : Kieren Fallon two-day ban: careless riding (Oct 9-10)

Analysis

GRAHAM DENCH

The Royal Lodge Stakes has a mixed record as a source of future stars, and the 2010 renewal – the last at Ascot before the race was transferred to Newmarket – appeared to lack strength in depth, but Frankel confirmed himself an exceptional talent by winning in a style that had to be seen to be believed.

Having been held up in last behind what looked an ordinary pace, he cruised past his four rivals rounding the home turn and sprinted right away again in the final two furlongs. While the ten-length runner-up Klammer was no star, he had been awarded a Deauville Listed race on his previous start and took the Group 3 Horris Hill Stakes on his only subsequent appearance. Third-placed Treasure Beach went on to be beaten only a head by Pour Moi in the Derby and win both the Irish Derby and the Secretariat Stakes.

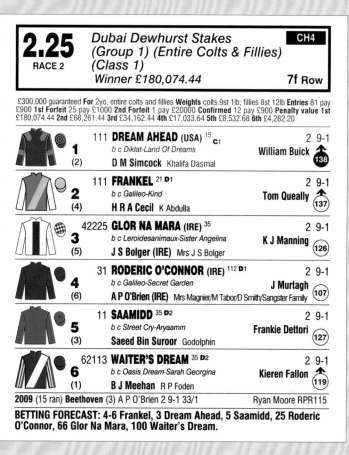

2.25 RACE 2

Dubai Dewhurst Stakes
(Group 1) (Entire Colts & Fillies)
(Class 1)
Winner £180,074.44

CH4

7f Row

£300,000 guaranteed **For** 2yo, entire colts and fillies **Weights** colts.9st 1lb; fillies 8st 12lb **Entries** 81 pay £900 **1st Forfeit** 25 pay £1000 **2nd Forfeit** 1 pay £20000 **Confirmed** 12 pay £900 **Penalty value 1st** £180,074.44 **2nd** £68,261.44 **3rd** £34,162.44 **4th** £17,033.64 **5th** £8,532.68 **6th** £4,282.20

1 (2)	111	**DREAM AHEAD** (USA) [15] c1 *b c Diktat-Land Of Dreams* **D M Simcock** Khalifa Dasmal	2 9-1 William Buick	138
2 (4)	111	**FRANKEL** [21] D1 *b c Galileo-Kind* **H R A Cecil** K Abdulla	2 9-1 Tom Queally	137
3 (5)	42225	**GLOR NA MARA** (IRE) [35] *b c Leroidesanimaux-Sister Angelina* **J S Bolger** (IRE) Mrs J S Bolger	2 9-1 K J Manning	126
4 (6)	31	**RODERIC O'CONNOR** (IRE) [112] D1 *b c Galileo-Secret Garden* **A P O'Brien** (IRE) Mrs Magnier/M Tabor/D Smith/Sangster Family	2 9-1 J Murtagh	107
5 (3)	11	**SAAMIDD** [35] D2 *b c Street Cry-Aryaamm* **Saeed Bin Suroor** Godolphin	2 9-1 Frankie Dettori	127
6 (1)	62113	**WAITER'S DREAM** [35] D2 *b c Oasis Dream-Sarah Georgina* **B J Meehan** R P Foden	2 9-1 Kieren Fallon	119

2009 (15 ran) **Beethoven** (3) A P O'Brien 2 9-1 33/1   Ryan Moore RPR115

BETTING FORECAST: 4-6 Frankel, 3 Dream Ahead, 5 Saamidd, 25 Roderic O'Connor, 66 Glor Na Mara, 100 Waiter's Dream.

Dubai Dewhurst Stakes

Newmarket, October 16, 2010

Frankel put himself in pole position to be champion juvenile as Racing Post *handicapper Simon Turner gave him a Racing Post Rating of 122+, which put him 3lb ahead of fellow two-year-olds Casamento and Pathfork, who both received a mark of 119.*

Jane Chapple-Hyam, the trainer of Royal Lodge runner-up Klammer, dubbed Frankel a 'freak' and Cecil revealed the Dewhurst Stakes was the preferred end-of-season target.

Frankel was now 2-1 or 5-2 favourite with every firm for the 2,000 Guineas, but there was more discrepancy where the Derby was concerned, with Coral and Paddy Power shortest at 5-2, but Ladbrokes, Totesport and bet365 offering 4-1.

Following Frankel's Royal Lodge demolition Casamento, Dream Ahead and Wootton Bassett showed that Cecil's star colt was not yet home and hosed for the 2,000 Guineas. Casamento was a four-length victor of the Beresford Stakes at The Curragh, Dream Ahead struck by an impressive nine lengths in the Group 1 Middle Park Stakes, and Wootton Bassett completed the set when a ready winner of the Prix Jean-Luc Lagardere at Longchamp on Arc weekend.

A week before the Dewhurst, Cecil said of Frankel: 'He still seems to be improving and has grown up a lot.

'He is in good order and seems to be maturing a lot and settling better. He wears a crossed noseband but we'll be able to take that off next year as he's doing very well and relaxing better. Since the Royal Lodge he's been making more and more progress.'

Cecil added: 'He's exciting all of us. We've got a lot of exciting three-year-olds but I don't get these sort of horses now.

'You go back to horses like Wollow and Diesis and he's as good a two-year-old as we have had over the past

few years and I don't know if we've had a two-year-old as progressive.

'It is nice to have a horse for the Dewhurst – we have been a bit thin on the ground over the last six or seven years. I appreciate it and I hate being an also-ran.'

Frankel continued to impress gallop-watchers in the run-up to the Dewhurst, but on the Wednesday before the race he made front-page news with a blistering piece of work.

The Post *posed the front-page question, 'The greatest two-year-old race ever?' on Dewhust day with Frankel due to lock horns with Dream Ahead and Saamidd.*

Tony Elves *was very taken by Frankel's midweek gallop:*

I have seen a lot of gallops over the years, and the one that Frankel delivered last Saturday was breathtaking. He worked with an older lead horse and just blew him away.

Tom Queally showed him some daylight, and, without being asked a question, he pulled ten lengths clear. The last horse I saw work like that was Eswarah before she won the Oaks in June 2005.

Sometimes you worry that a horse can leave a race behind on the gallops, but this went exactly as everyone would have wished and the horse was totally switched off afterwards.

Frighteningly for his opponents, he looks to have improved since the Royal Lodge. He seems to have matured and he settles a lot better as well. You just can't find a flaw in him.

I've seen a lot of Dream Ahead over the summer on the peat moss gallop, and in a normal year you would nail your colours to a horse who has won two Group 1 races in the style he has done.

A lot of Saamidd's work has taken place behind closed doors on Godolphin's private Chippenham gallop. We did get a glimpse of him when he had a racecourse gallop at Newmarket with two older companions, but that wasn't the breathtaking sort of work we've been seeing from Frankel and Dream Ahead.

Even so, Godolphin have been calling him Pegasus, and they aren't prone to making statements like that lightly.

What we've got in prospect is one of the races of the century and I am 100 per cent of the opinion that Frankel should be odds-on.

The way he gallops suggests that he is every inch a superstar. If I don't come away today having seen him confirm how very good he is, I'll be extremely disappointed.

Dewhurst day in 2010 was going to be a sad occasion for many at Newmarket as it would be the last time the Champion Stakes – first run there in 1877 – would be held on the Rowley Mile. From 2011 it would be run at Ascot to form the centrepiece of the richest fixture in British racing history.

The switch was engineered as part of the Racing For Change project that considered a £3 million Champions Day at a venue closer to London necessary if the sport was to compete for a wider audience.

Frankel confirmed he was the real deal in a Dewhurst romp to complete a perfect day for Cecil as Twice Over repeated the previous year's success in the Champion Stakes – as **Jon Lees** *reported.*

Frankel goes clear in the Dewhurst Stakes

The groundwork was undone in the first few strides but Frankel yesterday negotiated the hazards that threatened to puncture his enormous reputation and clinched the Dubai Dewhurst Stakes victory that prompted two bookmakers to take the unprecedented step of installing a winter favourite odds-on for the 2,000 Guineas.

Even though the Group 1 did not follow the script prepared for the 'two-year-old race of the century', with its two other principals Dream Ahead and Saamidd underperforming, Frankel remembered his lines, delivering a display that propelled him to 4-5 favouritism for next year's colts' mile Classic with William Hill and Coral, shorter odds than the likes of Xaar, Zafonic and Tudor Minstrel were at the same stage.

But while trainer Henry Cecil compared him to Arazi, there was a warning to those tempted to take a top price of 4-1 about Frankel for the Investec Derby that he may remain over a mile after the Guineas.

Much less spectacular than when landing the Royal Lodge Stakes by ten lengths, Frankel still beat Roderic O'Connor and Glor Na Mara by two and a quarter lengths and two and three-quarter lengths in a time 0.31 second quicker than that recorded earlier by Red Jazz, the year-older winner of the Victor Chandler Challenge Stakes.

Tom Queally had a job to restrain Khalid Abdulla's colt early on, a bump he received when Dream Ahead veered right exiting the stalls having set him alight, but Frankel moved up to challenge front-running Roderic O'Connor two furlongs out and dispatched his opponent without his jockey having to exert himself seriously.

'He quickened up well,' said Queally. 'He didn't need a smack. It felt as impressive as it probably looked. He got a bump on leaving the gate and it just sort of set him alight. He went to post a lot better today than he did in the Royal Lodge. There were spectators along the side and he was looking at them. I think the bump undid all the groundwork I had done from the time I jumped on his back but it shows the talent he has in reserve.

'It's great that he's won because there has been a lot of hype. It hasn't got to me but bubbles are always there to be burst.

'Henry has done a good job with him. When he looks back on Wollow and the good ones he's had, he's got the same high hopes for him. Let's hope he's right.'

Frankel returns to warm applause from the crowd at Newmarket

Xaar, Zafonic and Tudor Minstrel were even-money favourites for the Guineas after winning the Dewhurst and Frankel was available at 5-4 with Ladbrokes and evens with Paddy Power. He is 3-1 for the Investec Derby with Hills, 5-1 to complete the Guineas-Derby double and 10-1 to be unbeaten as a three-year-old.

Cecil, who received a rapturous ovation, said: 'If they had gone a bit faster and he hadn't got that bump he might have been more impressive. It's lovely to have a horse like this. At home he works unbelievably well. If he were a Formula One car he would win everything, as long as I didn't drive him.

'I have never had a horse, a two-year-old, work like him. The last horse I remember like this was Arazi, who was similar in some ways. This horse has got a lot of potential. Hopefully, he will have a good winter and everything goes right and he should make a lovely three-year-old. I am not going to do the usual thing for a trainer or tell the jockey to say he is the best horse they have ever ridden. That's all right for three-year-olds when they are going to stud. We have got a long way to go.'

Henry Cecil surrounded by the press after the Dewhurst Stakes

Cecil indicated Frankel would run in a prep race before the 2,000 Guineas, possibly the Greenham Stakes, but seemed cool on a Derby bid.

'I'm not clever enough to go for the Guineas without a prep. I don't trust myself,' he said. 'I'm not going to try and make him into a Derby horse if he's not going to stay.

'I am hopeful he will make a Guineas and St James's Palace horse. Whether he will get further later on in his life, we'll see but it will be up to the prince. I have to thank the prince for everything.'

Alastair Down *was again enraptured.*

Newmarket and its crowd have long belonged to Henry Cecil but never more so than yesterday when he had his greatest ever Rowley Mile afternoon courtesy of two Group 1 winners in the shape of the magnificently exciting Frankel and the oh-so-accurately named dual Champion Stakes scorer Twice Over.

Anyone expecting Frankel to exceed the dazzling impression he made at Ascot might have been fractionally disappointed but they shouldn't be because he was a very easy winner of the Dewhurst despite having pulled hard and wild through the first two furlongs. When the ever-cool Tom Queally asked him to make his ground to the outer Frankel did so with genuine ease and, never so much as touched with the whip, he forged unfussily clear to win by

FRANKEL

a two-and-a-quarter-length margin that was as decisive as it was comfortable.

Post-race both Cecil and Queally immediately pointed out that the bump and squeeze Frankel suffered after they left the stalls lit up the horse, thus undoing at a stroke all the work they have been putting in on the gallops to get him to settle. Given the energy he wasted fighting his jockey early, and the testing ground, this was a thoroughly meritorious performance by a horse who goes into winter quarters with every dream alive.

In a perfect world you would like to have seen Saamidd or Dream Ahead run closer to their form, but the Godolphin colt hated the ground and the Middle Park winner was simply never going with the fluency he has shown in his previous races.

David Simcock realistically conceded: 'He ran like a horse who has had one race too many for the season – his last run was only two weeks ago.'

Up in class, down in trip and on going with which he coped admirably rather than being suited by it, Frankel answered every question here. Some wonder whether his natural tendency to pull might get the better of him but he could hardly be in better hands. Just as they say 'fear travels down the reins', so it must be hoped that Cecil's unhurried serenity can be transmitted via that quiet voice and gently affectionate pair of hands over this coming winter of anticipation at Warren Place.

The trainer remains utterly convinced of his colt's exceptional quality. He said: 'I have never had a horse who worked like him. He is very settled at home – he lengthens and he's gone.'

That was certainly the impression here because while the 'whoosh and wow' element of Ascot was missing, there was something much more solid, bankable and believable about this performance.

In the Royal Lodge he was flashily impressive, but yesterday he left you with the indelible feeling that he could return in six months' time and outclass the best these islands can offer in the Guineas.

Mind you the quote of 4-5 for the first Classic will only tempt odds-on diehards and fanatics. One of the Big Three came up with 11-4 for Frankel to win both the Guineas and the Derby and the laughter was so loud they changed this actionable price to 5-1, horrible value for a horse whose post-Guineas target looks like being the St James's Palace Stakes.

Just under 40 minutes later Henry, whose outwardly calm demeanour masks a ferocious desire to be first, was back in the winner's enclosure after Twice Over took the Champion Stakes to crown the greatest ever year for Khalid Abdulla. Rarely, if ever, have I seen Henry make such a fatherly fuss over one of his charges and he revealed: 'He is my favourite horse.'

Indeed, Cecil was highly emotional following the Champion as he should have been because it is only those unsure of themselves who dare not let their inner feelings emerge in public every now and again. With that trademark hesitant eloquence he said: 'If it weren't for the prince I wouldn't be here. Just a few years ago I would have been at Catterick this afternoon.

'I am mentally in very good shape, I just wish my health was a bit better but I really do appreciate the crowd as they give me the will to go on.'

We all know the battles Cecil has fought in recent years as the sword of Damocles has hung, ever threatening, over him. And yesterday, at his spiritual home on the Heath, the crowd were determined to let him know for the umpteenth time just how deep their feelings run for him, roaring Twice Over back to unsaddle in a display of joyful solidarity with a man they hold in huge esteem.

I have said in the past that Henry may not have often set foot in a council house but remains revered by those who live in them. If some of the crowd's cheers were prompted by a desire to send the last Newmarket Champions Day out on an emotional high then there is nothing wrong with that. Next year we will gather for the purported climax to the season at Ascot, a course with its own micro-climate that includes the dark side of the moon where the sun has yet to shine.

That same sun has now set on Newmarket and it did so blazingly, casting the sort of roseate glow that warmed everyone there – autumn chill or not.

All winter we can look forward to Frankel, but the anticipation will not just be about the horse but also the extraordinarily complex, charismatic and triumphant character who trains him.

The good book exhorts: 'Let us now praise famous men', and Cecil is indeed that. But much more importantly he has long passed into the realm where we can describe him, foibles and all, as being our own.

After four runs and four wins Frankel moved back to the head of the two-year-old standings as Simon Turner awarded him a rating of 127 – the joint-best level which has been awarded to a winner of the Dewhurst – putting him 7lb clear of Roderic O'Connor and Wootton Bassett.

Turner wrote: 'This latest fine effort puts Frankel up to joint-third in the all-time top RPR two-year-old list behind Arazi on 134 and Celtic Swing on 133.

'Each time he has run, Henry Cecil's colt has left the impression there is better to come – an ominous sign for his rivals – and he heads into the winter break as one of the most exciting juveniles we have ever seen.'

The big question was whether Frankel would go to the Derby or not and Cecil issued a plea to punters the day after the Dewhurst.

'I don't think people should back him for the Derby – my advice is to sit and wait, because his chances of running in the Derby are probably less than 50 per cent,' he said.

'He might get a mile and quarter when he gets older but I don't see him at the moment as a Derby horse.'

Teddy Grimthorpe (right), racing manager to Prince Khalid Abdulla, receives Frankel's Cartier Award from Arnaud Bamberger in November 2010

The juvenile picture was further enhanced when Casamento won the Racing Post Trophy and Roderic O'Connor landed the Group 1 Criterium International at Saint-Cloud.

Frankel was crowned top two-year-old colt at the Cartier Awards and at the Racehorse Owners' Association awards. At the ROA awards Prince Khalid Abdulla was named owner of the year after a stellar season in which he won nearly £4 million in win and place prize-money in Britain and Ireland, with Cecil providing six Group 1 victories for his long-standing patron.

Prince Khalid's star colt was one of eight Group 1 winners for his sire and those victories enabled Galileo to regain the champion sire's mantle.

Frankel went into winter quarters at Warren Place as a red-hot favourite for Classic success in the 2,000 Guineas. Could he continue to justify the hype?

Following spread: *Frankel goes clear of Canford Cliffs and Rio De La Plata in the Sussex Stakes*

THE RESULT

6924	DUBAI DEWHURST STKS (GROUP 1) (ENTIRE COLTS & FILLIES)	7f

2:25 (2:26) (Class 1) 2-Y-O

£180,074 (£68,261; £34,162; £17,033; £8,532; £4,282) **Stalls** Low

Form						RPR
111	**1**		**Frankel**[21] 6347 2-9-1 123		TomQueally 4	127+

(H R A Cecil) *lw: hmpd sn after s: t.k.h: hld up in last pair: smooth hdwy ent fnl 3f: shkn up to ld over 1f out: in command whn rn green and edging rt fnl f: pushed out: comf* **4/6**[1]

	2	2¼	**Roderic O'Connor (IRE)**[112] 3469 2-9-1 0	JMurtagh 6	120

(A P O'Brien, Ire) *str: led: rdn ent fnl 2f: hdd over 1f out: drvn and btn 1f out: no threat to wnr but kpt on for clr 2nd fnl f* **25/1**

2225	**3**	2¾	**Glor Na Mara (IRE)**[35] 5975 2-9-1 0	KJManning 5	113

(J S Bolger, Ire) *w'like: scope: str: n.m.r and hmpd sn after s: chsd ldng pair: rdn and effrt ent fnl 2f: outpcd u.p over 1f out: kpt on same pce after* **33/1**

2113	**4**	hd	**Waiter's Dream**[35] 5943 2-9-1 109	KierenFallon 1	112

(B J Meehan) *chsd ldr: pushed along and pressed ldr ent fnl 3f: drvn and unable qck over 2f out: outpcd and wl hld fr over 1f out* **50/1**

111	**5**	1¾	**Dream Ahead (USA)**[15] 6531 2-9-1 128	WilliamBuick 2	108

(D M Simcock) *wnt rt and stdd s: t.k.h: hld up in last pair: swtchd rt and effrt over 2f out: rdn and hanging lft ent fnl 2f: no hdwy and wandered u.p over 1f out: sn wl btn* **5/2**[2]

11	**6**	10	**Saamidd**[35] 5943 2-9-1 115	FrankieDettori 3	82

(Saeed Bin Suroor) *hmpd s: t.k.h: hld up in midfield: rdn over 2f out: sn struggling: wl btn over 1f out: eased ins fnl f* **7/1**[3]

1m 25.73s (0.33) **Going Correction** +0.30s/f (Good)   **6** Ran   SP% 109.8

Speed ratings (Par 109): **110,107,104,104,102 90**

toteswingers:1&2:£3.00, 1&3:£5.80, 2&3:£14.20 CSF £20.07 TOTE £1.50: £1.10, £7.40; EX 17.50.

Owner K Abdulla **Bred** Juddmonte Farms Ltd **Trained** Newmarket, Suffolk

Analysis

GRAHAM DENCH

If there was a suspicion at the time that Frankel had not beaten much so far, there was no quibbling with the quality of the opposition he faced here, for among five opponents were Dream Ahead, a dual Group 1 winner who had beaten Strong Suit nine lengths in the Middle Park Stakes, Saamidd, also unbeaten and a good winner of Doncaster's Champagne Stakes, and solid representatives of the O'Brien and Bolger stables. Seldom has a two-year-old Group 1 been more eagerly anticipated.

In the event neither Dream Ahead nor Saamidd ran their race, but Frankel once again won in the style of an outstanding colt, despite the race not entirely going to plan after an early bump lit him up.

He took an uncomfortably keen hold through the first couple of furlongs yet made his ground smoothly and was in command with a furlong to go. The winning margin was much less extravagant than in the Royal Lodge, but he scored very comfortably and the form, which was questioned at the time, was franked just a fortnight later when runner-up Roderic O'Connor, the subsequent Irish 2,000 Guineas winner, took the Group 1 Criterium International at Saint-Cloud.

Frankel the three-year-old, 2011

3.10	totesport.com Greenham Stakes (Group 3) (Class 1)	CH4
RACE 4	Winner £28,385	7f Str

£50,000 guaranteed **For** 3yo colts and geldings **Weights** 9st **Entries** 8 pay £275 **Penalty value 1st** £28,385 **2nd** £10,760 **3rd** £5,385 **4th** £2,685 **5th** £1,345 **6th** £675

1 (1) — 411- **EXCELEBRATION** (IRE) 267
b c Exceed And Excel-Sun Shower
Marco Botti Giuliano Manfredini
3 9-0 Adam Kirby (111)

2 (3) — 1111- **FRANKEL** (TTF)182 **D2**
b c Galileo-Kind
Henry Cecil K Abdulla
3 9-0 Tom Queally (141)

3 (5) — 113- **PICTURE EDITOR** (TTF)168 **BF**
b c Dansili-Shirley Valentine
Henry Cecil K Abdulla
3 9-0 Ian Mongan (111)

4 (2) — 10- **SHROPSHIRE** (IRE) 241
gr c Shamardal-Shawanni
B W Hills The Hon Mrs J M Corbett & C Wright
3 9-0 Michael Hills (109)

5 (6) — 1132- **STRONG SUIT** (USA) (TTF)197 **C1**
ch c Rahy-Helwa
Richard Hannon Mrs J Wood
t 3 9-0 Richard Hughes (128)

6 (4) — 111-3 **VANGUARD DREAM** 21 **D1 CD1**
b c Oasis Dream-Garmoucheh
Richard Hannon Malih Lahej Al Basti
3 9-0 Ryan Moore (115)

2010 (5 ran) **Dick Turpin** (4) Richard Hannon 3 9-0 8/1 Ryan Moore RPR119

BETTING FORECAST: 1-3 Frankel, 7-2 Strong Suit, 20 Shropshire, 25 Excelebration, Picture Editor, 33 Vanguard Dream.

Totesport.com Greenham Stakes

Newbury, April 16, 2011

Frankel's Classic year began with the news in January that he only shared top billing with Dream Ahead when the World Thoroughbred Rankings were announced.

BHA juvenile handicapper Matthew Tester defended his decision to rate the two colts as joint champions, although he admitted he 'has trouble believing' that Dream Ahead will be a 126-rated three-year-old.

Cecil, who described Frankel as his most exciting two-year-old since his 1976 2,000 Guineas winner Wollow, was philosophical about the handicapper's verdict and said it was 'all a matter of opinion'.

Henry Cecil talks to Shane Fetherstonhaugh on Frankel (white star on forehead) on the Newmarket gallops on March 3, 2011

Frankel and Shane Fetherstonhaugh (centre) cross the Bury Road in Newmarket

More importantly, he reported that Frankel had wintered well and it was likely that his star colt would have his prep race for the Guineas in the Greenham Stakes at Newbury. Cecil added: 'People have blown him up into a wonder horse. Let's hope the bubble doesn't burst.'

As winter turned to spring, Frankel's development continued and at the end of March the Post *led on 'The Frankel Express. We're getting there – Cecil's verdict after his star colt outruns the 7.13 passenger service to Cambridge'.*

David Milnes *and* **Jon Lees** *reported:*

Frankel yesterday put paid to the old advertising slogan 'it's quicker by train' by outrunning the 7.13am passenger service from Newmarket to Cambridge, providing further compelling evidence his campaign for Classic honours is firmly on schedule.

That was not the only train he left in his wake, as the Guineas and Derby favourite scorched 20 lengths clear of lead horse Bullet Train in a workout which left trainer Henry Cecil declaring his potential superstar 'nearly there'.

The Al Bahathri Polytrack, which runs parallel to the Ipswich to Cambridge rail line, has been the scene of many failed equine attempts to lay up even with freight trains, but Frankel put on a show for the watching commuters, after which he was cut by Coral to 4-1 favourite (from 5) for the Investec Derby.

After having an easy weekend while Cecil was at the Dubai World Cup, Frankel was settled beautifully by Shane Fetherstonhaugh in a decent-paced spin and was still travelling powerfully at the business end of the seven-furlong exercise.

Frankel, generally odds-on for the Qipco 2,000 Guineas next month and cut for the Derby after featuring among the Totesport Dante entries, is set to work on the Limekilns grass gallop this weekend or next week, depending on the weather, before heading to the Greenham Stakes at Newbury on April 16.

Cecil said: 'I think Frankel is nearly there and the key with him is that he's now beautifully settled.

'Hopefully we can get him back on the grass before long but we desperately need some rain as the ground is still quite firm.'

Last year Cecil expressed doubts Frankel would stay the Derby trip, but having seen the colt become more relaxed over the winter, he included him among the five horses he has engaged in York's renowned trial for the Epsom Classic.

Late March 2011: Frankel and Shane Fetherstonhaugh exercise up Warren Hill

I thought he was very impressive. He looked the real deal. He almost ran too free early on but still quickened away from them. I liked the way he was very cool and calm beforehand too and he did everything right. He'll be hard to beat, no question.

ED DUNLOP
*trainer of 2,000 Guineas
hope Native Khan*

I thought Frankel looked fantastic for a horse who will improve for the race. He is a worthy favourite for the Guineas and he will be a hard horse to beat, but we may give it a go.

BARRY HILLS
*2,000 Guineas-winning
trainer*

It will take a very good horse to beat him in the Guineas. He was workmanlike today but last year he was exceptional. It is still early days for him but I hope he turns out to be a champion.

RICHARD HANNON
*three-time Guineas-winning
trainer*

For me he did it workmanlike. He wasn't brilliant but he was well on top at the finish and he'll no doubt come on for the run.

Owner Khalid Abdulla's racing manager Teddy Grimthorpe said: 'We have entered Frankel in the Totesport Dante, it being the best Derby trial.

'But how far he might stay has yet to be determined – Henry has said that the horse will tell us. First, Frankel will head to the 2,000 Guineas. We'll have to see what he does, how he does it and everything else at Newmarket, and go on from there.'

Although Cecil expressed some doubts the day before the Greenham Stakes about whether Frankel was ready for his reappearance because the dry spring meant he was unable to get any of his team on grass, the Guineas favourite came home four lengths clear of Excelebration, as **Graham Dench** *reported.*

It might not have had quite the wow factor that some were hoping for and there was even an anxious moment or two in the early stages when he looked as if he might not settle, but the further Frankel went the better he looked and those who have been nursing fancy ante-post prices for the Qipco 2,000 Guineas through the winter can breathe easily again.

So too can Henry Cecil, who confirmed that the dry spring had made the colt's preparation more difficult than he would have liked and admitted he had been nervous about the Royal Lodge and Dewhurst Stakes winner's reappearance in the Totesport-sponsored Greenham Stakes, a race he also chose for the reappearance of Wollow, another champion two-year-old, back in 1976.

Wollow won the Greenham before going on to land the Guineas. Frankel, who came home four lengths clear of the unheralded Excelebration in a race where second favourite Strong Suit was never well placed, is now as short as 4-9 with Victor Chandler to follow suit.

Cecil, who also ran Derby possible Picture Editor in the hope of ensuring a solid pace, described Frankel's return as 'very satisfactory' and said: 'Whatever he did today he'll come on a lot. The weather messed us up, as it's been so firm that I couldn't risk him on grass. This will do him the world of good. Hopefully it will put him spot-on for the Guineas.'

He added: 'The further he went the better. The pace wasn't really fast enough. Mine have been running well and getting tired, but he had the class to go to the end. He's not

Frankel shows his superiority over Excelebration in the Greenham Stakes at Newbury

quite there yet but hopefully he'll be 100 per cent in the Guineas. Everything considered, he did well.'

Jockey Tom Queally, who said that his opinion on Frankel's Guineas chance had not really changed as he has always been 'quietly positive' about it, added: 'Our lead horse wasn't really quick enough. I shouted at Ian [Mongan, on Picture Editor] to go on and at the same time gave mine an inch of rein and he dropped his head and settled. The biggest problem I had was pulling him up.

'He was obviously a little ring-rusty, but he did it nicely, and what I like is that there's something left in reserve as I didn't feel he was 100 per cent ready. He's dealing with things better now and taking it all in his stride. That's his trial and it's nice he's won it.'

Lee Mottershead *focused on the trainer:*

Even now, six decades into a career beyond compare, he continues to feel it. The sixties were still swinging when his first Group 1 winner was trained, but the passage of time has made it no easier for Henry Cecil to handle the anxiety and tension that go with days like this. Yesterday, on an afternoon whose significance was lost on no-one, Cecil felt the nerves. So did we.

He knew, and we knew, there was much more to be lost than gained. If Frankel's season develops as many hope it will, the Greenham Stakes will become no more than a small paragraph in his story. But on the day itself, it was an Everest that had to be climbed. Sent off at 1-4 he might have been, but Frankel went into Newbury's starting stalls with many of his most ardent fans strangely fearing the worst. You couldn't put a finger on why, but there was a tangible sense that the bubble could be burst. Thankfully it wasn't.

'If you don't get nervous you might as well pack up,' said Cecil in the Newbury winner's enclosure after the job had been done. The relief on his face was as tangible as the worry had been just a few minutes earlier. To have experienced it before makes it no easier to feel it again.

But Cecil does not deal with these days on his own. Devoted wife Jane is forever at his side, as she was when the training legend first entered Newbury's weighing room just after 1pm. Ever observant, she noticed her husband had a clump of hair sticking up at the back of his head. As a mother would to a young child, she licked three fingers and attempted to flatten the troublesome follicles. Cecil stood there patiently, well behaved and docile, just the opposite of Frankel through the first half of the Greenham. Yet for that Frankel could be excused. And if not as wildly impressive as some had wanted, he could be excused that as well.

For all the talk of passenger trains being outpaced on the Newmarket gallops, Cecil had been at pains to point out that Frankel was appearing at Newbury for a reason. The horse was not fully fit, a run was badly needed. Yet again Cecil was proved right. Through the first two furlongs of the Group 3 test, Picture Editor, Frankel's Derby-entered pacemaker, could not go quickly enough for his more illustrious stablemate. Tom Queally had to plead with Ian Mongan to accelerate up front, but Picture Editor's fastest was not fast enough for Frankel, who expelled valuable energy by fighting for his head.

Once Queally was allowed control of that head, Frankel loomed large alongside Excelebration two furlongs out and, although there was most definitely a moment when all seemed not to be well, he eventually strode out

Opposite: *After the Greenham: the bond between trainer and horse*

in thoroughly convincing fashion, assisted by the first whip flicks he has experienced. Sensational it was not, but satisfactory it was, and that was what Cecil had both hoped for and anticipated.

'He's still not quite there yet,' he said more than once. 'I knew he wasn't, but I hoped he would have the class,' added Cecil, pointing to a quality Frankel has in abundance. You sensed he was more than pleased with what he had just seen. You sensed Queally felt the same. 'He is an animal not a machine, though he's been compared to one,' said the rider. 'People compare him to planes and trains but he only has to beat horses. He doesn't need to win grands prix. The Guineas will do.'

To win that Guineas he is as short as 4-9 with Victor Chandler and 1-2 with Ladbrokes. Yet not everyone was completely convinced, not least Native Khan's trainer Ed Dunlop, who described himself as now 'more tempted to go for the Guineas' with his Craven winner. 'It's just a feeling,' he said, adding: 'I'm often wrong.'

Dunlop will not be offended to know many racing fans will wish him to be wrong. To see Cecil win the Guineas with a truly great horse would delight the trainer's vast legion of supporters. Those same supporters can also now dream of him winning the Investec Derby, although surely not with Frankel but the much-touted World Domination, who produced the perfect debut performance to win an often informative maiden. Take Frankel out of the equation and World Domination is now favourite for the Derby. Perhaps a worthy favourite as well.

But the Derby can wait. In just 13 days' time, all eyes will be on Newmarket to see a Guineas that revolves around one horse, a horse who could still be everything we want him to be. For Cecil, and for the rest of us, it will be a nerve-wracking fortnight. The reward, however, should be worth it.

THE RESULT

1405 TOTESPORT.COM GREENHAM STKS (GROUP 3)   7f (S)
3:10 (3:12) (Class 1) 3-Y-O

£28,385 (£10,760; £5,385; £2,685; £1,345; £675) **Stalls** Centre

Form					RPR
111-	**1**		**Frankel**[182] [6924] 3-9-0 126 .... TomQueally 3		119+
			(Henry Cecil) *lw: sn trcking ldr: qcknd to chal 3f out: led sn after: shkn up and edgd lft 2f out: drvn and qcknd clr fnl f: easily*	**1/4**[1]	
411-	**2**	4	**Excelebration (IRE)**[267] [4332] 3-9-0 89 .... AdamKirby 1		108
			(Marco Botti) *t.k.h early: trckd ldrs in 3rd: drvn and qcknd to chal wnr 2f out: styd on terms tl readily outpcd appr fnl f: clr 2nd best*	**25/1**	
10-	**3**	6	**Shropshire (IRE)**[241] [5219] 3-9-0 94 .... MichaelHills 2		92
			(B W Hills) *t.k.h: chsd ldrs: styd on to take wl hld 3rd fnl 2f*	**18/1**[3]	
11-3	**4**	1½	**Vanguard Dream**[21] [990] 3-9-0 95 .... RyanMoore 4		88
			(Richard Hannon) *t.k.h early: in rr: rdn and outpcd 3f out: drvn and styd on fnl f to take wl hld 4th nr fin*	**20/1**	
113-	**5**	1¼	**Picture Editor**[168] [7236] 3-9-0 99 .... IanMongan 5		84
			(Henry Cecil) *sn led: jnd by wnr 3f out: sn hdd: wknd fr 2f out*	**33/1**	
132-	**6**	hd	**Strong Suit (USA)**[197] [6531] 3-9-0 113 .... (t) RichardHughes 6		84
			(Richard Hannon) *stdd s: t.k.h in rr: sme hdwy to dispute wl hld 3rd ins fnl 2f: wknd over 1f out and hung rt ins fnl f*	**9/2**[2]	

1m 24.6s (-1.10) **Going Correction** -0.10s/f (Good)   6 Ran   SP% **115.0**
Speed ratings (Par 108): **102,97,90,88,87 87**
Tote Swingers: 1&2 £2.90, 1&3 £2.90, 2&3 £6.30   CSF £12.45 TOTE £1.30: £1.10, £5.30; EX 9.30.
Owner K Abdulla **Bred** Juddmonte Farms Ltd **Trained** Newmarket, Suffolk

Analysis

GRAHAM DENCH

A small field for Frankel's first three-year-old start, and the betting suggested the Richard Hannon-trained Strong Suit was his only realistic rival.

For the first time Frankel was assisted by a pacemaker, Picture Editor, in a bid to curb the hard-pulling tendencies so evident in the Dewhurst, but he was keen again, soon tugging his way into second place and taking it up with well over two furlongs to go. Frankel was never in any real danger, but while a wind issue prevented Strong Suit from running his race this was no cakewalk and outsider Excelebration made him work harder than expected before he pulled clear in the final furlong.

Some thought Frankel's performance was relatively workmanlike but Marco Botti insisted we should not underestimate the unheralded Excelebration. He was right too, for next time out Excelebration romped home seven lengths clear in the German 2,000 Guineas and in almost any other era he might have been a worthy champion miler.

3.10
RACE 3

Qipco 2000 Guineas (203rd Running) (Group 1) (Entire Colts & Fillies) (Class 1)
Winner £198,695

1m Row

£350,000 guaranteed **For** 3yo, entire colts and fillies **Weights** colts.9st; fillies 8st 11lb **Entries** 52 pay £1000 **1st Forfeit** 19 pay £1400 **Confirmed** 15 pay £1100 **Penalty value 1st** £198,695 **2nd** £75,320 **3rd** £37,695 **4th** £18,795 **5th** £9,415 **6th** £4,725

No	Form	Horse	Details	Jockey	RPR
1 (12)	112419-	**BROOX** (IRE) (TTF)180 **BF**	b c Xaar-Miss Brooks **E J O'Neill** (FR) G A Lucas	3 9-0 William Buick	125
2 (10)	1211-	**CASAMENTO** (IRE) (TTF)189 **D2**	ch c Shamardal-Wedding Gift **Mahmood Al Zarooni**[1] Godolphin	3 9-0 Frankie Dettori	135
3 (5)	0419-11	**DUBAWI GOLD** 21 **D1**	b c Dubawi-Savannah Belle **Richard Hannon** Andrew Tinkler	3 9-0 Richard Hughes	121
4 (1)	1111-1	**FRANKEL** (TTF)14 **D2 C1**	b c Galileo-Kind **Henry Cecil** K Abdulla	3 9-0 Tom Queally	141
5 (4)	11-	**FURY** (TTF)210 **C1**	gr/b c Invincible Spirit-Courting **William Haggas** Cheveley Park Stud	3 9-0 J Murtagh	124
6 (7)	41-2	**HAPPY TODAY** (USA) 17 **D1**	b c Gone West-Shy Lady **Brian Meehan** Jaber Abdullah	3 9-0 Martin Dwyer	116
7 (8)	12-	**LOVING SPIRIT** 197 **BF C1**	b c Azamour-Lolla's Spirit **James Toller** P C J Dalby & R Schuster	3 9-0 Robert Havlin	114
8 (11)	114-1	**NATIVE KHAN** (FR) (TTF)16 **CD1**	gr c Azamour-Viva Maria **Ed Dunlop** V I Araci	3 9-0 Olivier Peslier	127
9 (2)	111-	**PATHFORK** (USA) (TTF)231	b c Distorted Humor-Visions Of Clarity **Mrs John Harrington** (IRE) Silverton Hill Partnership	t 3 9-0 F M Berry	133
10 (13)	13414-2	**REROUTED** (USA) (TTF)17 **C1**	ch c Stormy Atlantic-Rouwaki **B W Hills** K Abdulla	b1 3 9-0 Michael Hills	123
11 (3)	3121-	**RODERIC O'CONNOR** (IRE) (TTF)181 **D1**	b c Galileo-Secret Garden **A P O'Brien** (IRE) Mrs Magnier/M Tabor/D Smith/Sangster Family	3 9-0 Ryan Moore	134
12 (9)	116-	**SAAMIDD** (TTF)196	b c Street Cry-Aryaamm **Saeed Bin Suroor** Godolphin	t 3 9-0 Mickael Barzalona	128
13 (6)	561245-	**SLIM SHADEY** 217	br c Val Royal-Vino Veritas **J S Moore** Phil Cunningham	3 9-0 Luke Morris	110

2010 (19 ran) **Makfi** (5) M Delzangles 3 9-0 33/1   Christophe-Patrice Lemaire RPR123

BETTING FORECAST: 8-15 Frankel, 6 Pathfork, 8 Roderic O'Connor, 12 Casamento, 16 Fury, Native Khan, 33 Saamidd, 40 Dubawi Gold, 66 Loving Spirit, 100 Broox, Happy Today, Rerouted, 200 Slim Shadey.

Qipco 2,000 Guineas

Newmarket, April 30, 2011

Frankel's status as odds-on favourite for the Qipco 2,000 Guineas strengthened two days after the Greenham Stakes when Godolphin's hope Dubai Prince was ruled out of the first Classic of the season with an injury.

And Wootton Bassett was the next rival to fall by the wayside after trainer Richard Fahey said the Newmarket Classic would come too soon for his colt. Dream Ahead would also miss the race as trainer David Simcock said he would be trained for the French 2,000 Guineas instead.

Frankel continued to impress on the gallops and, although he would have a pacemaker at Newmarket in the shape of Rerouted, Cecil was prepared to send his star to the front, as **Lee Mottershead** *reported in Guineas week.*

The talk of the town is that the Guineas is as good as won. Speak to Newmarket's cognoscenti and you'll be told that only a freak of nature, perhaps four-legged but more probably biblical, can stop Frankel from becoming a Classic winner on Saturday.

Around the streets where he lives there is an inevitability about what is before us, so much so that the hot topic has become not if he will win but in what manner – and Henry Cecil yesterday spiced things up beautifully by suggesting that it could be from the front.

If truth be told, Cecil would rather not be saying anything. 'I'll let him do the talking,' was his line prior to Frankel's victorious reappearance at Newbury. Were it possible, Cecil would let Frankel do the talking not only on Saturday but beforehand as well. Talking, however, is one of the few things that has so far seemed beyond Flat racing's new wonder horse.

'Not really,' answers Cecil half-jokingly when asked if he enjoys discussing Khalid Abdulla's unbeaten brute. Unfortunately for Cecil, at a Rowley Mile press conference staged to promote both the Qipco Guineas Festival and the Qipco British Champions Series that it launches, it is towards Cecil that all ears are pricked. Sheikh Fahad is here to explain why Qatar is pumping money into British racing, John Gosden is here to tell us that Sheikh Fahad is the sport's saviour and Jamie Spencer is here to tell us that he won't even be here on Saturday or Sunday.

In reality, though, everyone just wants to listen to Cecil and he says plenty of interest, not least on the subject of where Frankel will be positioned through the race. He makes clear his belief that Frankel's pacemaker Rerouted is no hopeless rag. Less obvious, however, is whether Cecil believes the pacemaker will be fast enough.

'I would like a decent, sensible pace, but if I don't get it I'm quite happy to do it myself,' says Cecil, who, intriguingly, made Frankel lead usual work companion Bullet Train during a Monday canter.

'We'll see how things pan out, but he could make the running if he had to – hopefully he won't have to. He has a very long stride, an extraordinary stride, and when you take a pull you take him out of his stride. On the other hand, if you let him go and allow him to use himself he relaxes. If the pace was wrong you wouldn't fight him. Why not just let him relax in front?'

Asked how confident he is that Frankel will be in front at the finish, Cecil – who maintains a wait-and-see line on the Derby – goes a tad coy.

'That's a very difficult question,' he says. 'At this stage I wouldn't swap him but there's no such thing as a racing certainty.'

He continues: 'At Newbury he was ready for a race but he wasn't tuned up. I've trained him for the Guineas and I'd like to think he will be a much better horse on Saturday than at Newbury.

'I admire people who can produce a horse on Guineas day first time out and win – that's fantastic but I don't think I could do it. In the old days you always used to give a horse a prep race before a Classic. That has changed, but I don't know why. John Gosden and I like the idea of a prep race but then we're practically Edwardian.'

Cecil goes back not quite that far, but he has been winning British Classics since 1975 when Bolkonski gave him a first 2,000 Guineas success. Should Frankel oblige on Saturday, Cecil's domestic Classic haul will total 25. No wonder, then, that he is walking his box. 'There is obviously a certain amount of pressure,' he says. 'You always worry a little bit about things going wrong. One goes through the other runners and tries to pick holes in them so you can forget about your own. I think that unless you have a few butterflies it's not worth doing.'

Aware of those butterflies, Newmarket has sought not to make things worse.

'We haven't overplayed the Frankel factor in our advertising,' says managing director Stephen Wallis. 'We would love him to win, but we don't want to load even more pressure on the human team behind the horse. They have enough pressure on them as it is.'

But at least Cecil once again has reason to feel pressure. Through his slump, he was not needed on days such as this. Now, master of his own renaissance, he once again has us hanging on his every word. 'I don't like being an also-ran,' he says. 'It would be awful to go out as a complete disaster.'

With Frankel at his side, there seems little chance of that happening.

The 2011 2,000 Guineas took place the day after the wedding of Prince William and Kate Middleton – thereafter the Duke and Duchess of Cambridge – and in expectation of a Classic romp for the hot favourite, the Racing Post *splashed with: 'KING IN WAITING – Racing world ready to hail a new superstar as Henry Cecil's Frankel puts his brilliant run on the line in the Qipco 2,000 Guineas at Newmarket'.*

Those who expected Frankel fireworks were not to be disappointed, and **Jon Lees** *described an astonishing race.*

After the royal wedding came a coronation at Newmarket yesterday when Frankel demonstrated he could be racing's new king with a performance as breathtaking as any occasion at Westminster Abbey.

The outstanding heir to a Classic title for the last six months, Khalid Abdulla's colt produced one of the most astonishing 2,000 Guineas-winning displays when making all the running to claim the Qipco-sponsored prize.

In a water-cooler moment for British racing, Frankel destroyed his field by six lengths, the second-widest winning margin in the history of the race, and bagged a 25th domestic Classic for his trainer Henry Cecil, plus a first in Britain for jockey Tom Queally.

Previous spread: *Frankel approaches the final furlong with a clear lead*

If there were any doubts about the colt's star quality after five wins, they were firmly laid to rest yesterday as Cecil and Queally executed the most audacious plan, wrongfooting their rivals – who expected Frankel to follow his pacemaker Rerouted – by letting him lead from the outset.

By halfway Frankel was so far clear that Queally took a peek between his legs and was reassured to see that no one was anywhere near him. He got to work on the colt with a furlong to run but victory was already secure and they passed the post to win by a margin bettered only by eight-length winner Tudor Minstrel in 1947. Frankel's starting price of 1-2 made him the shortest-priced winner of the race since Colombo scored at 2-7 in 1934.

Dubawi Gold beat Native Khan by a half a length for second with Slim Shadey 11 lengths clear of the next finisher Fury, while the race's other Group 1 winners, Pathfork, Casamento and Roderic O'Connor, could finish only seventh, tenth and 11th.

There followed a stampede from the stands to the winner's enclosure by awestruck spectators desperate to applaud Frankel.

'By God he showed them,' Queally said. 'He did it better than I ever thought he would. The first thing you think is what kind of speed we are going, but to Frankel it feels like a routine canter. Then he has quickened up and lengthened away. It's fantastic.

'I was amazed I was so far clear at halfway. He's happiest when he is galloping and I just wanted him to roll on. I felt at Newbury [in the Greenham Stakes] we were upsetting him holding him back and we maybe lost a length at the start we could have used at the end. We took them by surprise, but I'm delighted he did it like that.'

Cecil, who last won the 2,000 Guineas 35 years ago with Wollow, had hinted at making the running on Frankel earlier in the week so he could use his huge stride, a plan he finalised after the race draw, which berthed Frankel and Rerouted on opposite sides of the stalls.

'It worked out exactly as I wanted it to work out,' Cecil said. 'I thought he could do it like that if he relaxed from the front. Having been in front so long, he was wondering where all the other horses were. He was going to sleep and waiting for them, but that's not a bad thing.

'He hasn't taken too much out of himself. I thought if it was going to be a muddling pace I didn't want to put him

Frankel demolishes the 2,000 Guineas field, with Dubawi Gold and the grey Native Khan in vain pursuit

out of his stride. When I saw him six lengths clear I thought we'd done the right thing.'

Frankel was cut to a top-priced 7-2 for the Investec Derby with Victor Chandler, but is 6-4 with a run with William Hill and bet365. Having previously voiced doubts about the colt staying the Derby trip of 1m4f last year, Cecil declined to make any immediate commitment to Epsom.

He said: 'I have ideas, but we'll think. Once I have talked to the prince and we have worked it out together, then we'll let you know. He is in the Dante. We will see how he comes out of this and what we want to do.

'Whether he will get a mile and a half is another matter. If he was more of a miler, then there is the St James's Palace. We will leave all options open. If he is very well and he ran in the Dante we could easy bring him back a couple of furlongs at Ascot. We want to do the right thing and leave it completely open.'

Cecil was reluctant to compare Frankel to his other greats but was in no doubt he belongs in the same bracket.

'It's very difficult to put years together, different generations,' he said. 'We've seen some fantastic horses in our time. He must come into that category.

'Greatness is important for English racing too, for the public who love their racing to have a champion. We've

Tom Queally returns on Frankel after the 2,000 Guineas

had it with Arkle, Mill Reef, Sea The Stars and other horses. It's important to have something for everyone to look forward to.'

*And **Alastair Down** sang his own paean of praise:*

It has been an arid spring but something astounding blossomed on Newmarket's ancient Heath yesterday when Frankel put his Guineas field to beautiful rout in one of the definitive performances in the history of the turf.

Usually when you witness something utterly merciless it is cruel to watch, but not on this imperishable and joyous afternoon. They had not gone 200 yards when it hit you smack in the very marrow that the stuff of racing's future folklore was taking flight in front of us all as Frankel piled it on from the front and put his field contemptuously to the sword.

For a fraction of a second you just had to check with the rational part of the brain that Frankel hadn't taken charge of Tom Queally and was bolting to some ghastly oblivion. But there was no madness here, just the overwhelming sense of limitless power suddenly unleashed,

What they said

SIR PETER O'SULLEVAN
legendary commentator

Watching Frankel was just breathtaking and it was a spectacular performance. I can't remember another end-to-end Guineas win like that. It was so wise of Tom Queally not to restrain him; just hold him together and let him get on with it. It is not an orthodox way of winning the Guineas, but he was tactically absolutely correct to let things unfold and not to go out with any preconceptions.

SHEIKH MOHAMMED
owner and breeder

He is a great horse. We have not seen anything like that since Dubai Millennium won the Dubai World Cup. It was great to witness what he did.

PAT EDDERY
former champion jockey, won the 2,000 Guineas on Lomond, El Gran Senor and Zafonic

That was just awesome, and Frankel is exceptional. He is the best Guineas winner I've seen.

PAUL HANAGAN
champion jockey

Watching the race in the weighing room our jaws were on the floor. It was unbelievable to watch and great for racing.

avalanche-like, as he raced on a matchless even keel that had his rivals stunned stupid from stall-crash. Never before have I seen a top-class mile race over within two furlongs.

For months Henry Cecil and his team have husbanded the resources of this colt in a million for this day. And all praise to the trainer and Queally for keeping it so gloriously simple. No tactical complications, no 'what ifs', no soft options. They had the rare and raw courage to let Frankel go out and prove he was as spectacularly special as they believed him to be. Here was a colt who loves to run and to restrain him was to disappoint him – so they went the bold route and let him bowl along to utterly devastating effect.

In the paddock beforehand he got a touch warm but he gave you the impression of coiled power primed to deliver. And if Queally was brave in the race, he was faultless ahead of it, ceaselessly reassuring the Goliath beneath with endless pats, gentle fuss and chat in his ears. A man absolutely tuned in to the fact that Frankel could be vulnerable in the preliminaries in a way that he would never be in the race. You can't win a race in the paddock or on the way to post but you can lose it before it starts and the horseman in the jockey that is Queally was master of those tricky moments.

There is little I can tell you about the race itself other than to try to convey the magic as the air of vague disbelief turned to a wonderful certainty that he would indeed get home, imperious and unassailable, in a fashion that exceeded even the wildest hopes of all those who crave a great horse and love the majesty of an indisputable champion in full cry.

If there was a moment which defined the leagues by which Frankel was superior it came three furlongs out when Queally looked back between his legs to find out why it was so very quiet out in front with not a pounding hoof in earshot.

The glance told him he was a novice chase margin ahead and almost by instinct the jockey's hands came off his neck as he took half a pull on the powerhouse below him to conserve a touch of energy in case some marathon runner's wall reared up out of the blue in the run to the line.

The Rowley Mile is a wide, lonely place and bereft of reference points when a horse is a country mile clear, but Frankel never faltered and, with three judicious smacks to keep his mind on the job in hand, he ran home straight and true.

Opposite: *The aftermath*

By the time he hit the two-marker this was a victory parade. A performance as unimpeachable as this does not draw a visceral roar from those standing witness, but the climactic strides of this amazing Classic were played out to the soundtrack of thousands applauding because there was no better way to express both admiration for what we were watching and gratitude to be present on the day when the inner sanctum of the greats opened its ponderous doors to admit a new sensation.

We can leave it to the masters of ratings to quantify the undoubted enormity of what unfolded on the Heath yesterday. Pundits will draw fine distinctions and calculate things to an academic nicety. But to have been at Newmarket to see the performance and to join in the acclaim that greeted the revered Cecil and his crowning masterpiece that is this colt was to be part of something indelible and genuinely magical.

I cannot tell you what the future holds for Frankel but it would astonish me if the great days to come included a Derby or indeed any race over a mile and a half. But in a way I have not felt for years, I relish seeing this horse soar again on the racecourse for this trainer and jockey team and for the quiet architect that is Khalid Abdulla.

And over the whole mesmerising day stood the fragile colossus that is Henry Cecil.

I have always felt about this felicitous mix of the ruthless and the sensitive that we are indeed blessed to have shared his time and seen him reap the harvest of 25 Classics. And whatever stands to come for his trainer and this explosively brilliant colt we will, none of us, ever forget this satiating day God gave.

The Racing Post *'Topspeed' column gave the figures behind the performance.*

A stiff headwind put paid to any record time on the Rowley Mile but an explosive display of raw power saw his rivals just blown away. His time of 1m 37.30 seconds was over three seconds slower than the track record but scrutiny of the split times reveals the true merit of his visually stunning display. In a nutshell his electrifying display defied conventional wisdom.

When analysing the sectionals the usual caveats about hand times, points of reference and margin of error apply and from a standing start he covered the first furlong in 13.50, the second in 11.50, third 11.0, fourth 11.0 and fifth in 11.50 which cumulatively means he covered the first five furlongs in an astonishing 58.50 seconds.

Henry Cecil's highly polished performer went Group 1 sprinter's pace for the first five and his back-to-back 11-second sectionals saw him cover 20 yards each and every second. To put his long raking stride into perspective it is pertinent to recall that a cricket wicket measure 22 yards so he covered almost one each second during that high-octane quarter.

Put another way the time of the Palace House won by Tangerine Trees the same day albeit over a 'different' five was a second slower than Frankel who then maintained his relentless gallop for a further three furlongs.

Understandably he 'slowed' in the closing stages with the final three furlongs taking 12.5, 13 and 13.5 seconds respectively but factor in the headwind and the fact that he was in splendid isolation and overall his breathtaking performance on the clock is unlikely ever to be repeated.

THE RESULT

Analysis

GRAHAM DENCH

The smallest field since 1996, but while there were three notable absentees in Dream Ahead (who had shared top billing with Frankel in the official two-year-old rankings), Wootton Bassett and Dubai Prince, there was nevertheless credible opposition in the shape of fellow two-year-old Group 1 winners Casamento, Pathfork and Roderic O'Connor, plus Craven winner Native Khan.

Frankel had a different pacemaker this time in Rerouted, but when the pair were drawn on opposite flanks Tom Queally bravely elected to allow Frankel to bowl along in front. It was a move which took many by surprise – there was a suggestion that some jockeys initially assumed the clear leader was actually Rerouted – but it paid off in the most spectacular fashion, with 1 minute 37.30 seconds of pure magic, the like of which few on the Rowley Mile had ever previously witnessed.

In a ruthless display of controlled aggression Frankel was as far as ten lengths clear of the chasing Casamento by halfway and perhaps as much as 15 clear according to commentator Ian Bartlett's estimate by the Bushes. After galloping so hard from the start it would have been asking too much for him to maintain that kind of advantage to the finish,

but he remained in splendid isolation to the line, where his six-length margin over patiently ridden Dubawi Gold was the widest in the Guineas since the brilliant Tudor Minstrel scored by eight lengths in 1947.

Nobody was left in any doubt that Frankel had freakish ability,

the only question was in which direction it would be channeled. Opinions were divided, some suggesting dropping back to six furlongs for the July Cup and others begging connections to go for the Derby, but Royal Ascot's St James's Palace Stakes soon emerged as the next target.

1686 QIPCO 2000 GUINEAS (203RD RUNNING) (GROUP 1) (ENTIRE COLTS & FILLIES)
1m
3:10 (3:14) (Class 1) 3-Y-O

£198,695 (£75,320; £37,695; £18,795; £9,415; £4,725) Stalls Centre

Form				RPR
11-1	**1**		**Frankel**[14] 1405 3-9-0 126..TomQueally 1	133+
			(Henry Cecil) *warm: lw: sn led and clr: at least 10 lengths clr 1/2-way: rdn jst over 1f out: idling but kpt on fnl f: rdn out: unchal: impressive* **1/2**[1]	
0-11	**2**	6	**Dubawi Gold**[21] 1234 3-9-0 101................................RichardHughes 5	119
			(Richard Hannon) *lw: stdd s: hld up towards rr: hdwy 1/2-way: disputing modest 2nd and hung lft 2f out: chsd clr wnr over 1f out: kpt on but no threat to wnr* **33/1**	
14-1	**3**	1/2	**Native Khan (FR)**[16] 1341 3-9-0 111................................OlivierPeslier 11	118
			(Ed Dunlop) *sltly on toes: hld up off the pce in midfield: rdn and hdwy over 3f out: chsd clr wnr wl over 2f out tl over 1f out: kpt on but no threat to wnr* **16/1**	
245-	**4**	11	**Slim Shadey**[217] 6347 3-9-0 101................................LukeMorris 6	93
			(J S Moore) *lw: racd off the pce in midfield: rdn and sme hdwy whn hung rt over 2f out: wnt modest 4th jst ins fnl f: n.d* **200/1**	
11-	**5**	1/2	**Fury**[210] 6560 3-9-0 103................................JMurtagh 4	92
			(William Haggas) *w'like: cl cpld: racd off the pce in midfield: rdn and no real hdwy whn hung rt over 2f out: n.d* **12/1**	
41-2	**6**	5	**Happy Today (USA)**[17] 1320 3-9-0 102................................MartinDwyer 7	80
			(Brian Meehan) *sltyl on toes: s.i.s: bhd: sme hdwy over 2f out: n.d* **100/1**	
111-	**7**	3	**Pathfork (USA)**[231] 5975 3-9-0 120................................(t) FMBerry 2	73
			(Mrs John Harrington, Ire) *lengthy: athletic: lw: prom in main gp: rdn and no hdwy 1/2-way: no ch fnl 3f* **8/1**[2]	
14-2	**8**	1/2	**Rerouted (USA)**[17] 1318 3-9-0 110................................(b[1]) MichaelHills 13	72
			(B W Hills) *lw: chsd wnr for 2f: rdn 3f out: no hdwy and no ch after: wknd over 2f out* **66/1**	
12-	**9**	1 1/4	**Loving Spirit**[197] 6884 3-9-0 98................................RobertHavlin 8	69
			(James Toller) *hld up in midfield: rdn and short-lived effrt wl over 2f out: wl bhd after* **66/1**	
211-	**10**	8	**Casamento (IRE)**[189] 7081 3-9-0 119................................FrankieDettori 10	51
			(Mahmood Al Zarooni) *lw: chsd clr wnr after 2f: rdn and no hdwy over 3f out: lost pl and wl bhd over 2f out: t.o* **11/1**[3]	
21-	**11**	2	**Roderic O'Connor (IRE)**[181] 7265 3-9-0 119................................RyanMoore 3	46
			(A P O'Brien, Ire) *nt grwn: prom in main gp: rdn and struggling over 3f out: wl bhd fnl 2f: t.o* **8/1**[2]	
116-	**12**	14	**Saamidd**[196] 6924 3-9-0 115................................(t) MickaelBarzalona 9	—
			(Saeed Bin Suroor) *a in rr: nvr on terms: t.o fnl 2f: eased ins fnl f: fin lame* **22/1**	
410-	**13**	11	**Broox (IRE)**[180] 7277 3-9-0 112................................WilliamBuick 12	—
			(E J O'Neill, France) *cmpt: sltly on toes: awkward leaving stalls: sme hdwy into midfield 5f out: wknd over 3f out: t.o and eased fr over 1f out* **100/1**	

1m 37.3s (-1.30) **Going Correction** +0.30s/f (Good)   **13** Ran   SP% **123.5**
Speed ratings (Par 112): 118,112,111,100,100 95,92,91,90,82 80,66,55
toteswingers: 1&2 £8.40, 1&3 £4.40, 2&3 £35.70. CSF £34.53 CT £179.45 TOTE £1.40: £1.02, £7.10, £3.70: EX 28.20 Trifecta £238.10 Pool: £20,537.50 - 63.81 winning units..

Owner K Abdulla **Bred** Juddmonte Farms Ltd **Trained** Newmarket, Suffolk
■ Tom Queally's first Classic winner and Henry Cecil's 25th. The shortest priced 2000 Guineas winner since Colombo (2/7) in 1934.

3.45 RACE 3

St James's Palace Stakes (Group 1) (Class 1) Winner £141,925 1m Rnd

BBC2

£250,000 guaranteed **For** 3yo entire colts **Weights** 9st **Entries** 48 pay £850 **1st Forfeit** 23 pay £1050 **Confirmed** 13 pay £600 **Penalty value 1st** £141,925 **2nd** £53,800 **3rd** £26,925 **4th** £13,425 **5th** £6,725 **6th** £3,375 **Tariff** £160,000

1 (3)	1115-	**DREAM AHEAD** (USA) (TTF)241	3 9-0	
		b/br c Diktat-Land Of Dreams	William Buick	139
		David Simcock Khalifa Dasmal		
2 (7)	19-1122	**DUBAWI GOLD** 24 **BF D**1 **C**1	3 9-0	
		b c Dubawi-Savannah Belle	Richard Hughes	133
		Richard Hannon Andrew Tinkler		
3 (1)	411-21	**EXCELEBRATION** (IRE) 23 **D**1	3 9-0	
		b c Exceed And Excel-Sun Shower	Adam Kirby ▲	133
		Marco Botti Giuliano Manfredini		
4 (5)	1111-11	**FRANKEL** (TTF)45 **D**2 **CD**1	3 9-0	
		b c Galileo-Kind	Tom Queally	147
		Sir Henry Cecil K Abdulla		
5 (6)	711-431	**GRAND PRIX BOSS** (JPN) 37 **D**2	3 9-0	
		b c Sakura Bakushin O-Rosy Mist	Mirco Demuro	133
		Yoshito Yahagi (JPN) Grand Prix Co. Ltd		
6 (4)	212-813	**NEEBRAS** (IRE) 19 **D**1	3 9-0	
		b c Oasis Dream-Crossmolina	Frankie Dettori	125
		Mahmood Al Zarooni Godolphin		
7 (2)	3414-28	**REROUTED** (USA) (TTF)45	3 9-0	
		ch c Stormy Atlantic-Rouwaki	Michael Hills	122
		B W Hills K Abdulla		
8 (9)	11111-5	**WOOTTON BASSETT** (TTF)30 **BF**	3 9-0	
		b c Iffraaj-Balladonia	Paul Hanagan	134
		Richard Fahey Frank Brady & The Cosmic Cases		
9 (8)	61113-2	**ZOFFANY** (IRE) (TTF)16 **BF**	3 9-0	
		b c Dansili-Tyranny	Ryan Moore	129
		A P O'Brien (IRE) M Tabor, D Smith & Mrs John Magnier		

2010 (9 ran) **Canford Cliffs** (4) Richard Hannon 3 9-0 11/4J   Richard Hughes RPR123

BETTING FORECAST: 1-3 Frankel, 8 Excelebration, 12 Dream Ahead, Wootton Bassett, 14 Dubawi Gold, 16 Grand Prix Boss, 20 Zoffany, 66 Neebras, 150 Rerouted.

St James's Palace Stakes

Royal Ascot, June 14, 2011

Racing Post Ratings put Frankel firmly in the superstar category when Paul Curtis awarded him a mark of 133+, ranking him the best 2,000 Guineas winner since RPRs began in 1986.

Curtis wrote: 'That's an extraordinarily high figure for the time of year, but this was an extraordinary performance with an unconventional result and the sort of beaten distances that usually have no place in races like the Guineas.'

The following day Cecil all but ruled out the Derby for Frankel and suggested that the St James's Palace Stakes over a mile at Royal Ascot would be his next race.

Looking further ahead into what looked like a fascinating summer for British racing, trainer Richard Hannon was relishing the prospect of the possibility of his star miler and four-time Group 1 winner Canford Cliffs meeting Frankel. The Frankel camp were excited, too, about a clash with Canford Cliffs in the Sussex Stakes at Glorious Goodwood.

First, Canford Cliffs had a date with French supermare Goldikova in the Queen Anne Stakes at Royal Ascot and Frankel had his own race at the royal meeting to deal with.

Another accolade came Frankel's way after the Guineas when the official handicapper made him the joint-best racehorse on the planet.

To complete a remarkable renaissance for Cecil, he was awarded a knighthood in the Queen's birthday honours list, which the trainer said he was 'terribly grateful' to receive.

He added: 'I am terribly grateful to whoever was responsible for it and I'm more than slightly overwhelmed by the whole thing.

'I do feel quite funny knowing that I am receiving a knighthood. I always try to do my best and I thought if I did well in my profession people can't say I'm useless.'

The first three races on the opening day at Royal Ascot promised a real treat for racegoers with Canford Cliffs taking on Goldikova in the first race and then 75 minutes later Frankel running in the St James's Palace Stakes, with the best sprinters lining up in the King's Stand Stakes.

Cecil was confident that Frankel could extend his unbeaten sequence to seven, while Newmarket correspondent David Milnes couldn't see any other result than a Frankel victory.

However, it was far from plain sailing for Frankel as he just held on by three-quarters of a length – as **Jon Lees** *reported.*

Frankel's cherished unbeaten record came unexpectedly close to being shattered after an extraordinary run in the St James's Palace Stakes that forced the superstar's followers to endure a nail-biting climax.

The colt who had appeared so invincible in winning the Qipco 2,000 Guineas was made to look mortal as he held the closing Zoffany by less than a length in a fraught final-furlong finale to Royal Ascot's traditional first-day showpiece.

Trainer Sir Henry Cecil and jockey Tom Queally had outlined a plan to make a move for home before the home turn, but the resulting execution, under which Frankel was asked to close the big gap on flat-out pacemaker Rerouted after covering only three furlongs of the 1m race, left them vulnerable at the finish.

From holding a six-length advantage with two furlongs to run, the margin was narrowing quickly in the final 100 yards as Zoffany emerged from the chasing pack. But the move came too late to overhaul the 30-100 favourite, who edged home by three-quarters of a length, with Excelebration a length and a half back in third, to the obvious relief of Cecil.

'That was nerve-wracking,' he said. 'It didn't quite go to plan. The pacemaker went off at quite a decent gallop and after Frankel had won his race, rather like at Newmarket, he'd done enough.

'But he wasn't tired. I was getting really concerned at the end, because he was going to sleep, wasn't he?

'You can ride him very differently now. He has got a really long stride and he does kill horses, but I think you can sit a furlong and a half longer. There's nothing

Tom Queally galvanises Frankel in the closing stages…

left there, I was thinking to myself in the closing stages, but Tom said the horse idled on him.

'Frankel did everything right; he went down beautifully, but the race just went wrong for him. If you ran it again, the result would be very different. He's exceptional and hopefully he'll prove it again.'

Frankel earned the loudest ovation of the day after marking the weekend announcement of a knighthood for Cecil with the trainer's 73rd victory at the royal meeting and his fifth in the St James's Palace.

Queally said he was faced with a difficult dilemma when the rest of the field took no notice of the pace being set by Rerouted.

'I had to make a decision to move up,' he said, 'though we were going to do that anyway.

'He galloped and he lengthened when he went clear, and he's so good he was doing it easily. He wasn't tired, he was just idling.'

Despite the narrowness of the win Cecil still believes Frankel will get further than a mile and connections will contemplate whether to aim the colt at the Juddmonte

ROYAL ASCOT

... and the colt holds on by three-quarters of a length from Zoffany

International, sponsored by his owner-breeder Khalid Abdulla, or stay at this trip.

'It may be the Sussex or the Juddmonte but it's too early to say,' he said. 'The prince has never won the Juddmonte and he would love to, but let's do the best for the horse. Myself and [the owner's racing manager] Teddy Grimthorpe will advise him and he'll make the decision.'

The sense of anti-climax was shared by **Alastair Down**.

There were two processions scheduled for Royal Ascot yesterday. Her Majesty's went off without a hitch – she was first past the post as usual – but it was only Frankel's innate brilliance that got him home in a St James's Palace Stakes in which the Guineas winner did not so much flirt with disaster as almost jump into bed with it.

Although all's well that ends well and the engravers can duly etch the seventh consecutive victory on this exceptional colt's honour roll, this was a far closer-run thing than the three-quarter-length victory margin suggests.

When Henry Cecil said afterwards: 'I was getting really concerned at the end – it was a bit nerve-wracking,' he spoke for many of us who felt we had been dangled out of the window by the ankles more than was strictly necessary or advisable for those with a high cholesterol count.

And let's get one thing bang clear. This is a blinding colt, but the more you see him race the more you understand that he is anything but straightforward.

Cecil said of him: 'The horse is a gentleman but he is complicated. He's a very hot-blooded horse.'

Of course any muppet with a licence can train the easy point-and-go ones, but Frankel is an endless set of character issues like one of those Russian dolls which repeatedly reveals a new face. I am utterly sure that at the end of his career the thing for which we will give the most thanks will be the fact that he was in the hands of a man whose genius was more than match for his idiosyncrasies.

It should also be recorded that the reception given to Frankel when he returned to the winner's enclosure was the finest since they rebuilt the old pile and amid the cheers and resonating through the applause was admiration and affection for an exceptional colt and his irreplaceable trainer.

If some were slightly taken aback that Frankel has not won by a wide patch of empty Ascot sward then the reason for their surprise must lie in the tactics employed. There is much to be said for Tom Queally, but he surely had a

Tom Queally celebrates Frankel's Royal Ascot success, under the watchful eye of Henry Cecil's travelling head lad Michael McGowan

half-brother to a brainstorm when, fully five furlongs from home, he sent Frankel off in hot and high-risk pursuit of his pacemaker Rerouted, who was blazing along up front in the sort of isolation best ignored.

Frankel closed down Rerouted with all the ease you would expect and led entering the final three furlongs – indeed with two to run he was six lengths clear and the stands began to call him home in anticipation of the Guineas winner powering away like some hero in a children's book.

But at the very moment when the crowd began to get overexcited you started to suffer nagging doubts that this could all end in tears, and on my left-hand side arguably the best judge in Christendom intoned sagely: 'This is not over yet.'

Nor was it. Soon hard ridden, Frankel was being reeled in over the last 100 yards by horses he should have played with and he was all out to win by three-quarters of a length. Idling or not, there was no sleeve full of extra aces waiting to be played on this occasion.

Luckily, no damage was done and three-parts of a length is hardly the stuff of pixels. But it was perilous of the estimable Queally to fire Frankel up as early he did and I cannot believe he would ride the same race again if given the choice.

Even Cecil said: 'It didn't go to plan. He is growing up but it just went a little bit wrong today. If the race was run again in half an hour it would be very different.'

While nobody died, Frankel has now had two hard races in a row when probably only one was necessary. Cecil was right to be adamant that Frankel is proving more amenable to restraint as he gets older and more race-wise and when the trainer added: 'It means we can ride a normal race on him,' it almost sounded like a prayer.

And it must be said there was plenty of divided opinion over Frankel after the race. Chalking up a potential Sussex Stakes clash between Frankel and ultra-cosy Queen Anne winner Canford Cliffs, Ladbrokes went 8-11 Canford Cliffs, with Frankel at evens. Yet Coral priced up any eventual meeting of the two at 1-2 Frankel with Canford Cliffs out in the cheap seats at 6-4.

But it may be that Frankel is headed for the Juddmonte International, which is sponsored by Khalid Abdulla, who has yet to win the race. Certainly Queally was in no doubt that

*Cameras at the ready:
Frankel returns to the winner's
enclosure*

Frankel would get further and the ten and a half furlongs at York would be less of a pressure-cooker in terms of tactics.

Don't get me wrong – I was highly delighted Frankel won. But there is much to be said for the fact that he didn't do so by the sort of humiliating margin he posted in the Guineas because from now on there will be more horses prepared to run against him as his cloak of invincibility looked a touch more threadbare here.

After the hell-out-of-the-night charge up the Rowley Mile and then getting away with a tactical mish-mash here, it strikes me the only option now is to ride him like something he will never be – an ordinary horse. That's when normal service will be resumed – and he could well become extraordinary once more.

Again Topspeed provided the revealing details.

This was expected to be a lap of honour for Frankel but it did not materialise and, although visually the least impressive of his victories, the sectionals underline that he is truly the real deal.

Settled off a blistering early pace set by Rerouted, Frankel hotfooted after the leader much earlier than planned and was in front three from home. Again the caveats about hand-held sectionals apply but it would seem that he covered the third, fourth and fifth furlongs of Ascot's Old Mile in a collective time of 34.2 seconds suggesting that the alacrity with which he made up the ground possibly surprised Tom Queally as well as everyone else.

His finals splits were 11.9, 12.9 and a relatively sluggish 13.60 totalling 38.40 and by comparison his split for the equivalent section in the previous season's Royal Lodge was 35.60, practically three seconds quicker.

Most horses can sustain genuine acceleration for about two and a half furlongs or around 30 seconds and the later in the race they do it the better. The fact that Frankel expended his energy so early in proceedings but still won is the hallmark of an exceptional talent. Few if any horses would have won had they popped their cork so soon.

THE RESULT

Analysis

GRAHAM DENCH

There was real strength in depth here, with recent victims Dubawi Gold and Excelebration joined by European two-year-old Group 1 winners Dream Ahead, Wootton Bassett and Zoffany, plus another from Japan, Grand Prix Boss, but Frankel was long odds-on and few would contemplate defeat. However a combination of circumstances contrived to threaten Frankel's unbeaten record in the most dramatic finish of his career.

Although pacemaker Rerouted had gone off way too fast and was being widely ignored, Tom Queally elected to extricate Frankel from the pack and go after him with a good five furlongs still to go. Ridden to chase him down rounding the turn and head him with three furlongs still to go, Frankel was soon some six lengths clear, but this time he had been ridden with almost reckless aggression and it was soon obvious this

was not going to be another procession. Queally was hard at work from two out, and on the uphill finish the pack were rapidly whittling away the advantage. However, they never quite got to him, and at the line he had three-quarters of a length to spare over Zoffany, who had been last into the straight.

His record was preserved, but Racing Post Ratings had him 11lb below his Guineas mark.

RACECARD

3.10 RACE 3
Qipco Sussex Stakes (British Champions' Series) (Group 1) (Class 1)
Winner £170,130
1m

£300,000 guaranteed **For** 3yo+ **Weights** 3yo colts and geldings 8st 13lb; fillies 8st 10lb 4yo+ colts and geldings 9st 7lb; fillies 9st 4lb **Weight for age** 3 from 4yo+ 8lb **Entries** 35 pay £1000 **1st Forfeit** 12 pay £1500 **Confirmed** 9 pay £500 **Penalty value 1st** £170,130 **2nd** £64,500 **3rd** £32,280 **4th** £16,080 **Tariff** £160,000

3111-11 **1** (2)	**CANFORD CLIFFS** (IRE) (TTF)43 **D4** **CD1** b c Tagula-Mrs Marsh **Richard Hannon** The Heffer Syndicate, M Tabor & D Smith	4 9-7 **Richard Hughes**	(137)
14-6013 **2** (4)	**RAJSAMAN** (FR) 66 **D3** gr c Linamix-Rose Quartz **F Head** (FR) Saeed Nasser Al Romaithi	b 4 9-7 **Thierry Jarnet**	(127)
1211-34 **3** (1)	**RIO DE LA PLATA** (USA) (TTF)43 **D3** **C1** ch h Rahy-Express Way **Saeed Bin Suroor** Godolphin	6 9-7 **Frankie Dettori**	(126)
111-111 **4** (3)	**FRANKEL** (TTF)43 **D4** b c Galileo-Kind **Sir Henry Cecil** K Abdulla	3 8-13 **Tom Queally**	(142)

2010 (7 ran) **Canford Cliffs** (8) Richard Hannon 3 8-13 4/6F   Richard Hughes RPR130

BETTING FORECAST: 8-11 Frankel, 11-8 Canford Cliffs, 20 Rajsaman, 40 Rio De La Plata.

Qipco Sussex Stakes

Goodwood, July 27, 2011

The much-anticipated clash of the generations in the Qipco Sussex Stakes was on after Canford Cliffs's spectacular defeat of Goldikova in the Queen Anne Stakes and Frankel's narrow victory in the St James's Palace Stakes.

It was a marketing man's dream and Goodwood, as well as the sport as a whole and Racing For Change in particular built up the clash at the Glorious meeting as the 'Duel on the Downs' and the participants did what they could to promote the event, which would see Frankel meet older horses for the first time in his career.

Tickets sales were ahead of the previous year and both camps were confident of their chances while being respectful about the other.

Canford Cliffs's rider Richard Hughes said: 'I'm a huge admirer of Frankel. He's probably the best three-year-old over a mile in a long time. I'm not afraid to lose because Frankel is a brilliant horse. If I beat him it will be better but there will be no disgrace if he beats me; vice-versa for that matter.'

On the other side, Tom Queally added: 'Canford Cliffs is a high-class horse. He's proved himself at Goodwood before but Frankel is a very well-balanced colt and I can't see the track posing a problem.'

The homework continued in the same vein as it had throughout the year for Frankel, and Cecil decided to dispense with the services of a pacemaker for the Sussex, such was the improved attitude of the horse.

Newmarket correspondent David Milnes reported: 'Whatever tactics are decided, the rumblings from Warren Place suggest that Frankel is in better shape than he's ever been and could be about to raise an already high bar of performance to an even loftier perch.'

Ascot was soon forgotten as Frankel went into overdrive on the Sussex Downs. **Jon Lees** *was there.*

Sir Henry Cecil claimed Frankel was the best horse he had ever seen, and not one of the 19,000 people who packed

Frankel gets the better of Canford Cliffs in the 2011 Sussex Stakes

Goodwood yesterday would argue after having had the privilege of witnessing the most superb performance by the Qipco Sussex Stakes winner.

Cecil rated Shergar and Blushing Groom at his peak as special talents, but neither quite matched Khalid Abdulla's extraordinary three-year-old homebred, who in defeating Canford Cliffs confirmed to his 68-year-old trainer that he was 'definitely the best horse I've seen in my lifetime'.

Abdulla, whose previous champions include Dancing Brave, agreed, saying: 'I was hearing what Henry was saying about the horse and I thought that he was the best I had had.' He added Frankel could stay in training next year 'if Henry wants him'.

Frankel's career has been defined by a sequence of jaw-dropping displays, but until yesterday those seven consecutive wins had all been against horses of his own age.

A match with Canford Cliffs, the leading older miler and last year's Sussex Stakes winner, provided the true guide to his ability, and when the pressure was on neither Frankel nor his jockey Tom Queally were found wanting.

Queally, criticised for committing very early on Frankel in the St James's Palace Stakes at Royal Ascot, wanted to ride a hold-up race this time but was not allowed that luxury by any of his three rivals and had no alternative but to make the running.

This time the rise in tempo was gradual rather than sudden, but when Frankel hit top gear approaching the furlong pole Canford Cliffs was quickly outpaced, hanging badly left as the winner streaked to a five-length victory – the widest margin since 1949 – with Rio De La Plata and Rajsaman bystanders in third and fourth.

Asked afterwards if he was surprised to see Canford Cliffs struggling, Cecil replied: 'It's an awful thing to say, but no. I have great respect for Shergar and Blushing Groom at his best. They gave me the impression of being very out of the ordinary. The days of Tudor Minstrel were before my time, but I think Frankel is probably the best horse we've ever seen. I am very lucky.'

He added: 'We had two options today – we could either settle him behind or, if there was no pace, let him settle in front. He's grown up an awful lot and has relaxed.'

Cecil compared the nervous build-up to preparing for a dental appointment. If he was anxious, he had told Queally to keep calm.

He said: 'I told him to relax and get the horse to relax. Frankel has a tremendous turn of foot and will go on for three or four furlongs. I didn't want that today. I said start producing him two furlongs out and he'll go all the way to the line. When he quickens, he quickens fast. He kills them.

'I hate predicting things, but I was going to put a piece of paper in an envelope with 'by five lengths' on it and I was going to produce it after. It's the worst thing you could do, though, like seeing one magpie.'

After his Royal Ascot ride had come under intense scrutiny Queally said little in public in the build-up to the race, but yesterday's faultless performance lifted a huge burden off his shoulders.

'When you are riding a horse of his calibre you have everyone watching every move,' he said. 'It's the way it goes. I have to deal with it and I still wouldn't swap it for the world.

'There was huge hype but the minute I jump on Frankel's back I'm grand. He was amazing and I'm just very fortunate to play a small part in it.'

Despite Canford Cliffs's victory last year, his performance this time convinced Richard Hannon that the Richard Hughes-ridden colt is not entirely suited to Goodwood.

He said: 'Richard said he thought he was beat three out and he was never travelling on the downhill run. I know he won last year but even then I thought this is not his track.

'It could be that [Frankel] is unbeatable but I think we should have been closer. We will definitely have another go at him.'

Again **Alastair Down** *had just the right words.*

Brilliance was redefined on the Sussex Downs yesterday when Frankel changed forever our idea of what constitutes the exceptional. His performance confirmed him not merely the shining light among milers of the modern era but of all the ages that have gone before.

We came to watch a horserace and were blessed instead with a sublime coronation. At the heart of horseracing lies a centuries-deep search for something simple and yet as elusive as a will o' the wisp – pure unadulterated thoroughbred speed. And just under a furlong from home, in this most anticipated of all Sussex Stakes, that longed-for holy grail came to light in front of our eyes as Frankel kicked in a staggering burst of acceleration that none who saw it will ever be able to shake from their mind.

And all you need know in terms of quantifying this rampant colt's super-abundant quality is the judgement of the man who trains him. Without a speck of triumphalism and in the most matter-of-fact manner, Sir Henry Cecil simply said: 'He is the best horse I have ever seen.'

Tellingly, he added: 'He is much better now than earlier in the year.' And how has that state of affairs come about? For one reason – and one alone – Cecil.

Back on Guineas day there was still something raw and uncouth about Frankel, his mildly delinquent tendencies still untamed. So Cecil, knowing that Frankel, for all his achievements, was still a work in progress, was brave enough to let him blaze from the front in a display of sustained murderous pace that remains one of the most extraordinary sights I have ever seen.

After the Guineas many doubted Frankel would ever be amenable to restraint again, but they reckoned without Cecil. If you want to know why the word 'genius' habitually appears in the same sentence as the name Cecil it is because he can wreak changes in horses as no other man – and it is his patience, instinct and sympathetic spirit that have transformed the tearaway, force-of-nature Frankel of April 30 at Newmarket into the grown-up superstar who settled in front before his withering turn of foot felled his rivals like stalks to the scythe.

The diamond in the rough of the Rowley Mile had been chiselled and polished to something almost flawless and perfect by the end of July.

Sir Henry Cecil congratulates Tom Queally

There will have been many hands who have played a small part in raising Frankel up to this level but the handpicked massed band at Warren Place have only one conductor.

It is rare, even in a lifetime's racing, that you can be utterly sure that what you have just seen is without parallel, but descending the steps from the press room yesterday to join the buzzing throng surging towards the winner's enclosure you were surrounded by folk united in the happy certainty they had just been uplifted by the sort of greatness that spans the generations.

By the time Frankel returned, every conceivable vantage point had been taken and the winner was accorded a welcome not seen in many a summer with Cecil given three rousing cheers.

Khalid Abdulla was animated as never before, smiling fit to burst and swept along by the joyful depth of the chord this victory struck with the crowd.

If this was Cecil's finest hour and Frankel his greatest monument, this was also Abdulla's moment – a lifetime owning and breeding horses rewarded with this indelible day.

And high among the heroes of the hour has to be Tom Queally. Nobody was under more pressure than Queally, who has been the subject of some ferocious, possibly gratuitous, media scrutiny since Royal Ascot but has conducted himself with astounding grace under fire. He put not a foot wrong here, getting the perfect tune out of Frankel. Cecil said: 'I told Tom to relax as this horse has the most fantastic turn of foot. When he quickens, he quickens very fast.'

And that is the essence of Frankel. In the Guineas we saw him sustain a gallop of scarce credible ferocity, but here he displayed a blasting change of pace which has to be just one of the things that has had the Cecil team utterly in this horse's spell as he has put together this run of eight consecutive victories.

Connections of Canford Cliffs were adamant their star was not at his best and the way he hung across the course adds credence to that view, although Richard Hughes in particular was at pains not to take anything from the winner.

But the lesson is not that Canford Cliffs finished second. The breathtaking surge of speed Frankel plucked almost lazily out of his repertoire with less than a furlong to run would quite possibly have left all milers ever born no better than second.

It looks as if we will see Frankel once more this year in the Queen Elizabeth II Stakes and anyone who has not seen him run in the flesh should move heaven and earth to be there. It is a sporting imperative. If you are due to do something else that day like die or get married, then change your plans.

There are encouraging sounds that Frankel may stay in training next year which would be a fabulous extension of a golden career.

Man has been breeding thoroughbreds for over 300 years and every foaling is a key to the dream that this new life might have the whiff of immortality attached. And, of course, on hundreds of thousands of occasions it doesn't happen. But every blue moon something completely removed from the run of the mill is born with the power to rewrite record books and change perceptions of what is achievable.

Frankel is one such freak of genes and circumstance. We are fortunate to be the generation to coincide with him. And blessed beyond what any of us have the right to hope is that this horse's near savage superiority has had Cecil as its shepherd.

THE RESULT

4425 QIPCO SUSSEX STKS (BRITISH CHAMPIONS' SERIES) (GROUP 1)

1m

3:10 (3:12) (Class 1) 3-Y-O+ £170,130 (£64,500; £32,280; £16,080) **Stalls** Low

Form						RPR
-111	**1**		**Frankel**[43] [3011] 3-8-13 130.. TomQueally 3			137+
			(Sir Henry Cecil) *t.k.h but a under control: mde all: shkn up and readily qcknd clr over 1f out: r.o strly in n.d fnl f: impressive*		**8/13**[1]	
1-11	**2**	5	**Canford Cliffs (IRE)**[43] [3009] 4-9-7 127....................... RichardHughes 2			125
			(Richard Hannon) *lw: trckd wnr: rdn over 1f out: immediately outpcd by wnr and btn whn hung bdly lft fr 1f out*		**7/4**[2]	
1-34	**3**	2½	**Rio De La Plata (USA)**[43] [3009] 6-9-7 120..................... FrankieDettori 1			119
			(Saeed Bin Suroor) *a same pl: hld up in tch: rdn wl over 1f out: sn outpcd and wl btn 1f out*		**22/1**[3]	
6013	**4**	2½	**Rajsaman (FR)**[66] [2343] 4-9-7 117...............................(b) ThierryJarnet 4			114
			(F Head, France) *str: hld up in last: rdn 2f out: outpcd and wl hld over 1f out*		**22/1**[3]	

1m 37.47s (-2.43) **Going Correction** 0.0s/f (Good)

WFA 3 from 4yo+ 8lb 4 Ran **SP%** 107.0

Speed ratings (Par 117): **112,107,104,102**

CSF £1.88 TOTE £1.90; EX 2.10.

Owner K Abdulla **Bred** Juddmonte Farms Ltd **Trained** Newmarket, Suffolk

Analysis

GRAHAM DENCH

The smallest Sussex Stakes field since Sallust beat two rivals in 1972, but the older Canford Cliffs's five successive Group 1 wins, the latest from outstanding French mare Goldikova in Royal Ascot's Queen Anne Stakes, confirmed him Frankel's toughest rival. With the St James's Palace scare fresh in the memory Frankel looked more vulnerable than ever before, especially on such an idiosyncratic track, and one which his rival was already proven on. Anticipation could hardly have been keener.

With no pacemaker and none of the others keen to lead Queally had little option but to make the running, and Frankel was soon setting a sensible pace, just running a shade keen, with Canford Cliffs no more than a couple of lengths behind.

The moment of truth came approaching the furlong-marker, when Queally asked Frankel to extend. The response was electric and the race was over in a matter of strides.

Canford Cliffs spoiled his finishing effort by drifting alarmingly left under pressure, and it emerged afterwards that he had suffered a career-ending injury. However, most acknowledged that even at his brilliant best he would have been hard pressed to trouble Frankel, who was simply stunning.

3.35
RACE 4

Queen Elizabeth II Stakes
Sponsored By Qipco (British Champions Mile) (Group 1) (Class 1)
Winner £567,100

BBC1

1m Str

£1,000,000 guaranteed **For** 3yo+ **Weights** 3yo colts and geldings 9st; fillies 8st 11lb 4yo+ colts and geldings 9st 3lb; fillies 9st **Weight for age** 3 from 4yo 3lb **Entries** 31 pay £3500 **1st Forfeit** 14 pay £3250 **Confirmed** 10 pay £3250 **Penalty value 1st** £567,100 **2nd** £215,000 **3rd** £107,600 **4th** £53,600 **5th** £26,900 **6th** £13,500 **Tariff** £160,000

1 (4)	10655-7 **BULLET TRAIN** TTF 184 **D1** b c Sadler's Wells-Kind **Sir Henry Cecil** K Abdulla		4 9-3 Ian Mongan	(124)
2 (5)	-149171 **DICK TURPIN** (IRE) TTF 21 **D4 C1** b c Arakan-Merrily **Richard Hannon** John Manley		4 9-3 Christophe Soumillon	(134)
3 (1)	19-2073 **POET'S VOICE** TTF 22 **D2 C1** b c Dubawi-Bright Tiara **Saeed Bin Suroor** Godolphin		t 4 9-3 Frankie Dettori	(127)
4 (8)	-311314 **SIDE GLANCE** 27 **D3 C1 CD1** br g Passing Glance-Averami **Andrew Balding** Pearl Bloodstock Ltd		4 9-3 Jimmy Fortune	(130)
5 (3)	1226414 **DUBAWI GOLD** 34 **D2 C1** b c Dubawi-Savannah Belle **Richard Hannon** Andrew Tinkler		3 9-0 J Murtagh	(130)
6 (7)	1-21311 **EXCELEBRATION** (IRE) 34 **D2** b c Exceed And Excel-Sun Shower **Marco Botti** Manfredini, Tabor, Smith & Magnier		3 9-0 Jamie Spencer	(137)
7 (2)	11-1111 **FRANKEL** TTF 80 **D5 C2** b c Galileo-Kind **Sir Henry Cecil** K Abdulla		3 9-0 Tom Queally	(148)
8 (6)	2-40111 **IMMORTAL VERSE** (IRE) 61 **D3 C1** b f Pivotal-Side Of Paradise **Robert Collet** (FR) R C Strauss		3 8-11 Gerald Mosse	(137)

2010 (8 ran) **Poet's Voice** (7) Saeed Bin Suroor 3 8-13 9/2   Frankie Dettori RPR123

BETTING FORECAST: 1-3 Frankel, 11-2 Excelebration, Immortal Verse, 20 Dick Turpin, 40 Dubawi Gold, Poet's Voice, 50 Side Glance, 100 Bullet Train.

Queen Elizabeth II Stakes (sponsored by Qipco)

Ascot, October 15, 2011

After the 'Duel on the Downs' Cecil shelved plans to take Frankel to York for a clash with Coral-Eclipse winner So You Think in the Juddmonte International Stakes, in what would have been his first race over further than a mile.

Instead, Cecil gave the inaugural Qipco Champions Day a huge promotional boost by declaring that he was more likely to give the colt a rest until the October 15 end-of-season finale at Ascot.

With Arc weekend at Longchamp and the Breeders' Cup firmly marked on the racing calendar, British Champions Day was the sport's response in this country. As well as being supported by Cecil, fellow trainers, owners and jockeys welcomed the move to provide a grandstand finish to the Flat season. The trainer also hinted that Frankel would race on as a four-year-old, when there would be a very good chance he would get a mile and a quarter.

Following the Sussex Stakes, Paul Curtis gave Frankel a Racing Post Rating of 137, which left him rated behind only Sea The Stars (138) among the best three-year-olds since RPRs began.

Of the elite three-year-olds on RPRs only Generous (137) achieved his figure in midsummer, with Sea The Stars, Peintre Celebre (137) and Zilzal (137) all improving through the year and posting their peak efforts in the autumn.

Having finished second to Frankel in the Greenham Stakes and third to him in the St James's Palace Stakes, Excelebration boosted the overall form with a six-length win in the Group 2 Hungerford Stakes at Newbury in the middle of August and he followed that up with victory in the Group 1 Prix du Moulin de Longchamp.

Across the Channel, Robert Collet was preparing Immortal Verse for a clash with Frankel in the Queen

*Elizabeth II Stakes after his filly had collected the
Coronation Stakes at Royal Ascot and the Prix Jacques
le Marois at Deauville.*

*Frankel was ticking over on the gallops during his
midsummer rest in preparation for Champions Day, which
Cecil was eager to support.*

*He said: 'It's an important event – the highlight of the
end of the year – and there are a lot of pluses about it. The
idea with Frankel is that he has the one race and we will
put him away for next year.'*

*As September went by Cecil was gradually bringing
Frankel back to his peak and he revealed that his star
colt was now under round-the-clock CCTV surveillance
with a monitor placed in his trainer's bedroom, where he
could check that his hot-blooded colt did not cause himself
an injury.*

In the middle of September **Brough Scott** *spent a day
with those who knew Frankel best, the people who kept the
super-charged wonder horse at his peak while trying to
satisfy his gigantic appetite.*

Frankel is not an elephant but he's always in the room.
For even as we hurried off to help Aideen Marshall feed the
fillies' yard in the moonlit dark of Warren Place at 4.30am
on Wednesday, the biggest thought was whether all would
be well when Chris Russell pulled the door in Frankel's
box across the paddock.

*Dee Deacon with Frankel's
breakfast*

FRANKEL

Team Cecil at Warren Place

It was. This year it always has been. Frankel's appetite is one of his key ingredients but so too – even from those first muffled greetings under the clear harvest moon – is the whole rhythm of life that beats through the yard of Sir Henry Cecil as it closes on the great Champions Day showdown at Ascot just four weeks over the horizon.

There are over 120 horses at Warren Place and more than 50 people would be present (and 16 absent) for the team photo we were organising later. Facts are that some team members, whether four-legged or two, are definitely more equal than others, yet everyone's effectiveness is imperilled if there is not involvement from the very bottom. And on Wednesday that started with the cats.

Tabby and Tiny are a long way short of their colleague Felix when it come to mice – let alone rat-catching – but Aideen, wife of assistant trainer Mike Marshall, cannot start the early morning duties she shares with Chris Russell, Dee Deacon and Peter Emerson until the moggies have been fed. 'Today's runners first,' says Aideen as, cats pacified, we lug the food trolley out into the moonlight. About eight boxes along she stops and puts a head collar on the rather

Mike Marshall with Sir Henry Cecil as Frankel warms up in the covered ring

opinionated incumbent so that it will walk to the manger rather than step out of the door.

This is Principal Role, a talented if slightly quirky performer who needs to win Yarmouth's big race this afternoon to maintain her exalted stabling right next to the Breeders' Cup heroine Midday and two away from the yard's other Group 1 filly Timepiece. We move the trolley through the dark to what looks like an aircraft hangar but turns out to be the Oh So Sharp Barn, named after Cecil's Triple Crown winner of 1985. 'I love feeding the fillies,' says Aideen, sensing the atmosphere of skittish feminine welcome so different from the horny snorting you get as a bunch of colts demand their breakfast.

The two runners who are to be fed first, light and leggy three-year-olds Asterism and Chabada, are the one pair who turn their noses up at the bowl of specially bruised oats with its handful of chaff and lovely juicy carrot which the others so enjoy. Both fillies petulantly spurn Aideen's offering and resume chattering through the partition, for all the world like two anorexic, over-bred girls at private school. Aideen can only compare not condemn as she moves to worthier recipients. 'She's pretty good,' she says of Midday, as the £2 million winner accepts her feed with aplomb if not gratitude, 'but she likes her own space – you wouldn't want to push her too far.'

These equine insights, including the observation 'thorough madam' about one inmate whose name we will withhold, are the privileges of early morning as is the sight, at 4.50am, of the trainer himself wandering through the darkness. As always he is a figure of languid, slightly rumpled chic with a mixture of quizzical interest and aloof pensiveness as he restlessly looks at lists, talks to staff, studies horses and indulges in a monologue of rhetorical musings which it seems best not to interrupt.

'With 16 people away there's hardly any point in the photo, is there?' he says. 'We worked the horses yesterday so they'll be doing just one canter today, it's easy to overdo it, isn't it?'

He is 68 now and, having taken over Warren Place from his father-in-law Noel Murless in 1976, has been padding round these boxes ever since, summer or winter, clear or damp, healthy or sick. Watching him so evidently enlivened by the environment makes it still scarcely credible that only six years ago the stable had shrunk to a 12-winner season and that this is the first year since the lean days that the whole of Warren Place has been filled with Cecil horses without the need for a supportive tenant.

But he doesn't like to dwell in the past, he is fuelled by planning the future. 'The paper makes So You Think 6-4 for the new Champion Stakes,' he says, 'ours [Twice Over and Midday] are third and fourth favourite. We [Frankel] are 1-3 for the Queen Elizabeth and the other mare [Vita Nova] is third favourite for the fillies' race. It's difficult, but they should run well, shouldn't they?'

Back in March there was something slightly shocking in the way his self-deprecating modesty switched to high-vaunting ambition, stating 'we were fourth last year [in the trainers' championship] but we could have been third. We could do it this time. Don't you think?'

He's fourth again at the moment but close enough for a glory day at Ascot to wrest back a championship he has ten times made his own. [Cecil went on to finish third behind Richard Hannon and Aidan O'Brien.] As the target looms closer he will say it less but those around him know it's the desire that drives him.

'He involves everyone. That's what is so special about him,' says Dee Deacon as she mixes the afternoon and evening feeds. 'This is his life and he's still so driven that it keeps him going and all of us too.'

Having been at Warren Place for 14 years and a head girl for the last three, Dee has seen good times and bad. 'With all he was going through,' she says of the toxic mix of personal and health problems that so nearly brought Cecil down, 'you couldn't imagine how he would manage, but he never missed a morning, however bad he looked. Sometimes we have had to hide our feelings to keep him strong and while he watches over us we watch over him too. It's deeper than a normal work relationship, it works both ways.'

Dee is mixing what seems to be a standard food bowl. She stirs a handful of molasses-sweetened chaff into the plastic tub of golden Canadian corn whose husks have been slightly bruised by the crushing machine to aid equine digestion. There is boiled bran and electrolytes to add, along with the usual vitamin, calcium and joint supplements that equine athletes take. It doesn't seem any different to the rows of others until you notice the quantity and then check the name on the wooden tag. This is Frankel's evening feed and, surprise, surprise, he eats more than all the others.

'Yes he just loves his food,' says Dee. 'Like the others he will have a bowl first thing and a couple of bowls at dinner time, but for the evening feed he'll take three good bowls of this Canadian corn. No other horse eats as much as that, but nothing fazes him. I remember when he came back after winning the Guineas he was already hollering for his food. It's obviously part of his secret.'

Quite what makes a champion is the oldest but most renewable topic in sport. Asking how Frankel compares with past Warren Place champions is like asking senior Old Trafford hands how Wayne Rooney rates against George Best and Bobby Charlton.

Billy Aldridge is drawing down oats from the crushing pipe in the ceiling. He teamed up with Cecil back in the 1970s and has ridden alongside all the stars. He ponders the sheer impossibility of the question and puts up Oh So Sharp's achievement of winning from 1m to 1m6f, before the intriguing personal comment 'she was bossy in her own way'.

Sunrise: Frankel and Shane Fetherstonhaugh before working on the Rowley Mile

He then adds Kris – the superb, albeit Classic-defeated miler of 1979. 'He was a hell of a good horse,' says Billy. 'Should have won the Guineas. Joe Mercer gave him too much to do.' But that's the past. Frankel is the present. There are lists to check, boxes to clear, horses to tack up, races to win. That's the actual point of it.

It's half past six by the time the string begins to gather at the big, circular, covered ride. Cecil and Mike Marshall stand side by side, one tall and willowy, the other short and firm. Much is noticed, little said. Frankel comes across with exercise rider Shane Fetherstonhaugh deep in thought, probably as much Frankel's as his own. A filly with a hood over her ears suddenly plants her forelegs and refuses to go forward. It is the Sun Chariot entry Chachamaidee.

Martyn Peake is one of those quiet, cool riders the stable cherishes. He leans forward and pats his filly's neck while the trainer walks over, puts a big, firm hand on the bridle and Chachamaidee walks smoothly on, the knot in her mind unravelled. It was a classic Cecil mix of almost feminine sensitivity and unmistakable masculine authority. No words were spoken but the exchange was eloquent.

Sir Henry Cecil and Mike Marshall after Frankel's workout on the Rowley Mile

It was a 40-strong first lot last Wednesday and as Frankel and his half-brother and lead horse Bullet Train came down Warren Hill at their accepted place at the head of affairs you could see both the pleasure and the pain he gives his trainer. 'I can be quite nasty you know,' Cecil says with an only half-joking laugh at the suggestion that snapper Edward Whitaker might go too close. The restless pacing to and fro (not to mention the quick drag on the cigarette) becomes even more contrastingly marked against the leisurely stalking walk which is Frankel's own hallmark.

The mood lifts as we trek across the heath to watch the string swing up the Warren Hill Polytrack. 'He's doing very well,' Cecil says of Frankel. 'Now he's learned to settle he would get a mile and a quarter. He'd get it now – even better next year.'

Frankel is only cantering up behind Bullet Train but the memory goes back a week to the vision of him streaking clear on his return to the grass gallop of the Limekilns. Beside Cecil, the young Italian Marco Botti shakes his head as he accepts congratulations for Group 1 victory in France with Excelebration, twice a vain pursuer of Frankel this season. 'That's my clever strategy,' laughs Botti to Cecil's teasing. 'Avoid Frankel.'

There's plenty of teasing at breakfast too, along with the quick crossword, the ever present entry book, the large, bound horse folder, and the home-grown fruit and vegetable health concoction which Lady Jane Cecil strains each morning and to which Cecil grudgingly concedes the benefit while wiping the beetroot stains from his mouth. 'It must be good for me,' he says, 'because I'm still alive, or at least I think I am.'

Goat's milk is also on his diet and the talk suddenly turns to a filly called Juve who had a goat as a companion way back in the 1970s but contracted grass sickness so badly that the owner ruled she should be put out of her misery. 'I went round to the box,' remembers Cecil in that vivid, almost childish way of his. 'She was lying down and looked dreadful, her eyes cloudy, her mouth creamy. But she looked up at me in such a way that I said I just can't do it now, I'll wait until the afternoon. You will never believe it but when I came back she was on the mend and she went on to win five races.'

It's a shaft from the past which holds in the mind as we go to see the two-year-olds on second lot. Among them is Noble Mission, who has to carry the somewhat unfair burden of being Frankel's full brother. 'He's had some sore shins and a few little problems,' says his trainer, 'but he's coming along and will probably run next month. He's not Frankel but he could be all right.'

Many of these won't run this season as Cecil uses the privilege of his experience to give them the time to develop their talent. Many will turn out to be no good, but one or two just may prove to be diamonds in the dross. That's the all-absorbing dynamic of the training game, but its dark side clouds in as we again walk over the heath to watch the canter.

First, Cecil sympathises with Peter Chapple-Hyam for his beaten odds-on shot the previous day at Yarmouth only to also hear that in a later race the trainer had a colt so badly struck into that he will have to be put down. Cecil has had his own brushes with mortality and the mournful look remains as Gay Jarvis rides up with difficult news about her much-loved husband Michael and his own battle with illness.

At moments like this those two-year-olds on the gallop are just young horses cantering up a hill – but they carry dreams with them, and dreams can be a treatment too.

The most potent on Wednesday seemed to be the filly Epoque, who winged easily up the Polytrack under Cecil's sister-in-law Sally Eddery in preparation for a first racecourse appearance, when third at Newmarket yesterday.

She promises the future, but as we later gather in the main yard for a team photo we are celebrating the present and the excitements of the immediate past. Dan de Haan, the big powerful horseman son of Corbiere's Grand National-winning partner Ben de Haan, rode Frankel through his formative, and at times tempestuous, first season. It was he who last spring found a way of anchoring the potential runaway and it was he who first felt the horsepower that may lay claim to be the greatest of them all.

'To start with all I was thinking of was trying to get him to settle and go straight,' says Dan, as vets and farriers and secretaries and dogs are rounded up in the grudging-smile

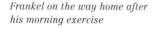

Frankel on the way home after his morning exercise

way of these things, 'but then one morning we went down to the Al Bahathri [all-weather gallop]. I took him up on his own and suddenly realised what was beneath me.

'Frankel is not actually that big – with me on him he looks quite small, but when you sit on him he feels as massive as Denman and the power beneath is just incredible. When I came back Mike [Marshall] said "What's that like?" and I said "It's an absolute beast. It could be anything".'

As we swung off the roundabout into Newmarket High Street the hands on the clocktower showed 11.30am – exactly seven hours after our headlights stabbed through the dark, driving up Warren Hill. Morning was ending but for the stable the day would stretch through the afternoon into the night. At 3.20pm Principal Role did a bit to justify her exalted box position by cruising clear in Yarmouth's race of the season; an hour later the two-year-old Feelthedifference drew clear at Beverley, and finally the Kempton floodlights looked down on those two food-faddish girls last seen spurning breakfast, Asterism and Chabada, as they finished first and third.

'It's been a good day,' says Marshall as he celebrates with his wife and mother-in-law later that evening. It had been but he knew, and we all know, that none of it will be enough until 'The Elephant' has done his stuff at Ascot.

Cecil said a week before Champions Day that Frankel was 'stronger than ever' and 'peaking at just the right time'. He added: 'He's relaxed, he's getting stronger, he's in really good order. Now that he is settled he can be with his leader [in this case his long-serving lead horse Bullet Train] and then let him go two and a half furlongs from home. The main thing about Frankel is that he quickens for a long way. From two furlongs down he will go right to the line and when he lengthens like that, other horses are not going to stay with him, are they?'

Although Frankel would be the star attraction on Champions Day, he would not have the limelight to himself as six of the world's top nine racehorses would be on show. In addition to Cecil's star colt, Nathaniel, So You Think, Cirrus Des Aigles, Excelebration and Twice Over were all set to line up. Although it was an important day for British racing, it took place against the backdrop of a set of controversial whip rules.

Tom Queally crouches low as Frankel goes into overdrive

In November 2010 the British Horseracing Authority, with the involvement of the Professional Jockeys Association and the RSPCA, began an examination into the effectiveness of whip rules and penalties. Following the 2011 Grand National, after winning rider Jason Maguire was banned for five days for hitting Ballabriggs 17 times in the run-in, the BHA announced a review of the whip rules with the intention of implementing the new rules from October 10.

New, harsher rules came into force in October and on the first day two jockeys received five- and ten-day bans. Within days the BHA said it would consider the views of the jockeys, who were increasingly up in arms. The day before Champions Day the riders threatened to go on strike at the two Flat meetings on the following Monday.

The Racing Post *splashed on Champions Day with* 'FRANKEL – An extraordinary horse for a special day', *and he proved himself once again with a thoroughly dominant performance.* **Jon Lees** *was on the spot.*

On a day for champions Frankel was in a class of his own as the race meeting billed the greatest show on turf saluted the greatest horse on turf at Ascot yesterday.

From ground level to fourth floor every vantage point of Ascot's towering grandstand was taken to hail Qipco British Champions Day's headline act after he had delivered a faultless performance in the Queen Elizabeth II Stakes.

If not quite as spectacular as previous displays, Frankel still dismissed Excelebration and Immortal Verse with complete authority, signing off a campaign that has yielded victories in the 2,000 Guineas, St James's Palace Stakes and Sussex Stakes with a four-length win that took his unbeaten record to nine.

Yesterday's performance could have been compared to a piece of work in Newmarket as Bullet Train, Frankel's regular lead horse, went off in front, opening up a substantial lead over the rest of the field. Tom Queally bided his time until moving Frankel forward approaching two furlongs out and once they hit the front they were never challenged.

'I know him so well and have great belief in him,' said Queally. 'I can give them as much rope as they want and he gets low to the ground and pegs them back. He's very easy to ride. The biggest job I have is getting him to the start, keeping him relaxed and talking to him, making sure everything is okay.

'This is the people's horse now. If someone asked me to sum up my season it would be one word – Frankel. He is amazing. I am very lucky.'

Judged by the volume of the roar from the crowd of 26,700, Frankel has a substantial following, one that is likely to grow next year when he stays in training, a season for which trainer Sir Henry Cecil has even greater expectations.

'He is a very good horse,' said Cecil. 'He was lovely and relaxed today. It's been a long year. He did everything I asked of him and I'm delighted. I'm really looking forward to having another winter with him next year when I'm sure he will get a mile and a quarter very easily.

'Today he was just doing enough. We weren't trying to catch pigeons, we were trying to win the race nicely and that was it. I was nervous. There is no such thing as a certainty, but everything went right.

'As long as he stays right he will be very exciting for next year. He is definitely a brilliant horse and hopefully he will

improve and we can judge him as time goes on. It's good for racing to have stars and champions.'

Frankel's owner-breeder Khalid Abdulla said afterwards: 'Many people think he is the best horse there has ever been so I am glad to have that horse. I hope he will do the same thing next year.'

William Hill offered a quote of 3-1 for Frankel to remain unbeaten through 2012, a season for which his choice of targets will be a source of much discussion until revealed by connections.

Excelebration suffered his third defeat at the hands of Frankel, a result trainer Marco Botti said was 'no disgrace'.

'We have to be proud of Excelebration,' he added. 'He tried his best but was second to a great horse. We've tried to beat Frankel three times and it has been no different each time.'

Botti said his colt was unlikely to run again this year, while another finished for the season is Immortal Verse, three and a half lengths off the second but whose preparation was hampered by a minor setback.

'For 11 days before the race she had to be led in hand so her preparation didn't go to plan as she was missing a bit of work, but I don't regret running,' said trainer Robert Collet. 'Frankel won the race so easily that even if we had been 100 per cent we would not have won.'

Alastair Down *caught the mood.*

He has gone from wild child to sober grown-up – a trajectory through life almost exactly mirroring that of his much-loved trainer – and at Ascot yesterday Frankel lit up the stage that could have been built for him when knocking them dead for the ninth time of asking with a clinical dismissal of his field in the Queen Elizabeth II Stakes.

There were no mid-race dramas and not so much as a scintilla of doubt as they powered up Ascot's straight mile, a venerable stamping ground for the thoroughbred but one which has probably never played host to a greater racehorse. Even when his pacemaker was a good ten lengths clear at halfway, Frankel moved with massive ease, Tom Queally's attuned fingers holding back the bowstring prior to unleashing the powerhouse beneath.

Early in the season you watched Frankel with your heart in your mouth, but now that nagging fear that he could implode or explode has gone, to be replaced by the fathoms-deep pleasure of watching something you know to be utterly exceptional. And one of the most striking things about being at Ascot yesterday was the sheer number of people who had made the journey solely to see this horse in the flesh and racing in anger.

We know he will be with us next season but racehorses, however much touched by the gods, are fragile things and ever the heir to accident. That is why, on this day of glittering prizes, you kept running into jumping nuts making sure they had seen him just the once, folk from the far north well off their beaten tracks and racegoers shepherding children who might in decades to come remember the perfect autumn afternoon when they were taken to Ascot to witness a phenomenon.

When Frankel began to reel in Bullet Train the crowd suddenly sensed the moment, and by the time he led imperiously just inside the two-pole all was acclamation – applause and cheers belting out of the vast barn of a grandstand as the crowd revelled in the occasion.

He wasn't doing a whole lot in front and connoisseurs of judicious use of the whip pointed out that when Queally notched a couple into him with 100 yards to run the great horse knuckled down and went again.

And as never before at Ascot those who had made it their business to be here for Frankel made a mass beeline for the usually soulless concrete desert of the unsaddling enclosure that was suddenly transformed into a place of genuine celebration. And, of course, while Frankel and Queally were still out front parading in front of the stands there was Sir Henry Cecil in the winner's zone and the crowd roared their approval of a man who has passed through some fires to stand here on this day with this extraordinary horse.

There is no doubt that a huge part of the public's attachment to Frankel is a function of their deep affection for Cecil. There just seems something so right that Frankel has come to him – and not in the early formative years of his career but towards the end. There is something magic about the dawn but something more lasting and memorable about the sunset.

And as we waited for Frankel and Queally to return it was worth drinking in the scene. Every stepping around Ascot's answer to the exercise yard at Alcatraz was rammed with folk, and up on the balconies at the back of the stand thousands of hands were raised, shielding eyes from the low autumn sun, as they strained for a glimpse of the winner returning.

When Queally brought him through they cheered and clapped him to the echo and, many minutes later after a lap of honour, the crescendo of thanks and sheer admiration rose again as the gladiator made his exit.

What struck you with real force, after Cecil had raised the roof for the umpteenth time as he went up to collect his trophy, was that everyone on course yesterday realised the rarity of Frankel, the singularity of him.

In my lifetime only Brigadier Gerard, with his 17 wins out of 18 runs, could be put up against this horse over a mile, and to those under 40 the Brigadier is like a figure from the middle ages.

Queally put it very simply: 'I don't think I will be on a horse like this again.'

No you won't Tom, not if you live longer than Methuselah – and that Old Testament pilot rattled up 969 years before he died a week before his grandson Noah went in the Ark.

At the beginning of this week we all wanted Frankel to win and by the end of it we all needed him to do so. That we have him to look forward to for another year is perhaps more than we deserve.

And so after days of depressing headlines, when sane outsiders had every right to ask if we had a brain between us as we made sure British Champions Day was blotted out in terms of news coverage by the whip, Frankel and Cecil in effect got us out of jail.

There will be time enough for post-mortems on an undoubtedly successful day, although I doubt Christophe Soumillon will recall it with joy unconfined after his six strokes of the whip in the final furlong of the Champion Stakes worked out at just over £9,000 a whack.

It can be an expensive game, this racing.

It was the perfect end to a perfect season as Frankel maintained his sparkling 100 per cent record, and Paul Curtis gave him a provisional Racing Post Rating of 139+, matching Dubai Millennium's 2000 Dubai World Cup romp as the highest recorded since RPRs began.

Ten days after Ascot, Frankel's brother Noble Mission made his debut at Yarmouth and finished a promising second over a mile.

Teddy Grimthorpe receives Frankel's HWPA President's Award on behalf of Prince Khalid from Steven Cargill at the Derby Awards Lunch in London

As the awards season loomed once again, Cecil went to Buckingham Palace in early November to receive his knighthood from the Queen, admitting it was 'the biggest honour I'll get in my lifetime'.

Frankel himself was crowned Horse of the Year at the Cartier Awards, as well as being named Horse of the Year by the Racehorse Owners Association. At those awards Khalid Abdulla was named owner of the year after a stellar 2011, which as well as Frankel's exploits included a third successive Nassau Stakes victory for Midday and Twice Over's victory in the Juddmonte International Stakes.

Cecil spoke at the ROA awards: 'I'm absolutely thrilled, very honoured and quite really taken aback to receive the award on behalf of Frankel. He couldn't be here tonight but he told me to tell you that he is very much looking forward to seeing you next year.'

THE RESULT

6860 QUEEN ELIZABETH II STKS SPONSORED BY QIPCO (BRITISH CHAMPIONS MILE) (GROUP 1)   **1m (S)**

3:35 (3:42) (Class 1) 3-Y-O+

£567,100 (£215,000; £107,600; £53,600; £26,900; £13,500)   **Stalls** High

Form					RPR
1111	**1**		**Frankel**[80] 4425 3-9-0 135... TomQueally 2		**139+**
			(Sir Henry Cecil) *lw: t.k.h early: hld up tl moved through to go 2nd 1/2-way: clsd to ld wl over 1f out and sn clr: reminders ins fnl f: r.o powerfully*		**4/11**[1]
1311	**2**	4	**Excelebration (IRE)**[34] 5988 3-9-0 126........................ JamieSpencer 7		129
			(Marco Botti) *sweating: hld up: prog fr 1/2-way: rdn to take 2nd over 1f out: r.o wl but vain pursuit of wnr*		**6/1**[2]
0111	**3**	3 1/2	**Immortal Verse (IRE)**[61] 5129 3-8-11 121...................... GeraldMosse 6		118
			(Robert Collet, France) *s.i.s: hld up in last: prog 2f out to chse ldng pair over 1f out: no imp: jst hld on for 3rd*		**7/1**[3]
6414	**4**	nk	**Dubawi Gold**[34] 5988 3-9-0 117... JMurtagh 3		120
			(Richard Hannon) *racd in 3rd to 1/2-way: outpcd and struggling 3f out: n.d after: styd on fnl f*		**28/1**
0101	**5**	3/4	**Dick Turpin (IRE)**[21] 6369 4-9-3 122.................... ChristopheSoumillon 5		118
			(Richard Hannon) *racd in 2nd to 1/2-way but ignored pcemaker: taken alone to nr side rail and struggling 3f out: no ch fnl 2f: kpt on nr fin*		**14/1**
2003	**6**	1/2	**Poet's Voice**[22] 6298 4-9-3 114.................................(t) FrankieDettori 1		117
			(Saeed Bin Suroor) *hld up in rr: prog whn inclined hd towards Excelebration at 1/2-way: rdn over 2f out: sn btn*		**33/1**
1314	**7**	hd	**Side Glance**[27] 6204 4-9-3 115.. JimmyFortune 8		116
			(Andrew Balding) *plld hrd early: hld up in rr: rdn and struggling in last over 2f out: no ch after*		**50/1**
55-0	**8**	2 3/4	**Bullet Train**[184] 1342 4-9-3 106... IanMongan 4		110
			(Sir Henry Cecil) *lw: led: drew 10 l clr after 2f: hdd & wknd wl over 1f out*		**150/1**

1m 39.45s (-1.15) **Going Correction** +0.125s/f (Good)

WFA 3 from 4yo 3lb   **8** Ran   SP% **115.8**

Speed ratings (Par 117): **110,106,102,102,101 100,100,98**

toteswingers:1&2:£1.80, 2&3:£2.00, 1&3:£1.70 CSF £3.06 CT £6.86 TOTE £1.40: £1.02, £1.80, £1.50; EX 3.90 Trifecta £7.00 Pool: £49,011.44 - 5,121.28 winning units..

Owner K Abdulla **Bred** Juddmonte Farms Ltd **Trained** Newmarket, Suffolk

■ Stewards' Enquiry : Jamie Spencer four-day ban: careless riding (Oct 29,31, Nov 1-2)

Analysis

GRAHAM DENCH

In a race switched to Ascot's straight course for the inaugural Qipco Champions Day there were four individual Group 1 winners to challenge Frankel, including new rivals Immortal Verse, Trumpet Major and the previous year's winner Poet's Voice.

Once again, however, it was one-way traffic once the keen-going Frankel was given his head and allowed to lead the pack in pursuit of his new pacemaker, sibling Bullet Train. He was in front inside the last two furlongs and in complete charge through the final furlong, chased home at a respectful four lengths by old rival Excelebration.

While visually not his most breathtaking performance of the year, the strength of the opposition was such that it earned him an RPR of 139, the best recorded on turf since the *Racing Post*'s inception and matched only by Dubai Millennium in that extraordinary Dubai World Cup win back in 2000.

Frankel the four-year-old, 2012

RACECARD

3.40 RACE 5 — *JLT Lockinge Stakes (British Champions Series) (Group 1) (Class 1)* Winner £99,242.50 — 1m Str

£175,000 guaranteed **For** 4yo+ **Weights** colts and geldings 9st; fillies 8st 11lb **Entries** 20 pay £600 **1st Forfeit** 14 pay £650 **Confirmed** 9 pay £500 **Penalty value 1st** £99,242.50 **2nd** £37,625 **3rd** £18,830 **4th** £9,380 **5th** £4,707.50 **6th** £2,362.50 **Tariff** £160,000

1 (5)	655/78-	**BULLET TRAIN** 217 **D1** b h Sadler's Wells-Kind Sir Henry Cecil K Abdulla	Ian Mongan	5 9-0 (124)
2 (2)	1444-04	**DUBAWI GOLD** (TTF)22 **D2** b c Dubawi-Savannah Belle Richard Hannon Andrew Tinkler	Jimmy Fortune	4 9-0 (135)
3 (7)	13112-1	**EXCELEBRATION** (IRE) (TTF)27 **D2 C1** b c Exceed And Excel-Sun Shower A P O'Brien² (IRE) D Smith, Mrs J Magnier, M Tabor	J P O'Brien	4 9-0 (143)
4 (6)	/11111-	**FRANKEL** (TTF)217 **D6 C1** b c Galileo-Kind Sir Henry Cecil K Abdulla	Tom Queally	4 9-0 ▲(153)
5 (3)	25188-9	**RANSOM NOTE** (TTF)30 **D4** b h Red Ransom-Zacheta Charles Hills H R Mould	Kieren Fallon	5 9-0 (132)
6 (1)	613110-	●**STRONG SUIT** (USA) (TTF)196 **C1** ch c Rahy-Helwa Richard Hannon Qatar Racing Limited	Richard Hughes	4 9-0 (140)
7 (4)	655-031	**WINDSOR PALACE** (IRE) 12 **D1** b h Danehill Dancer-Simaat A P O'Brien (IRE) D Smith, Mrs J Magnier, M Tabor	Seamie Heffernan	v¹ 7 9-0 (121)

●**STRONG SUIT** will run only if the ground is suitable, states trainer

2011 (7 ran) **Canford Cliffs** (4) Richard Hannon 4 9-0 4/5F   Richard Hughes RPR126

BETTING FORECAST: 1-3 Frankel, 3 Excelebration, 10 Strong Suit, 40 Dubawi Gold, 66 Ransom Note, 100 Bullet Train, Windsor Palace.

JLT Lockinge Stakes

Newbury, May 19, 2012

Twelve months on from the controversial decision to make Frankel and Dream Ahead joint champion juveniles, there was only one winner when the World Thoroughbred Rankings were announced at the start of 2012: Frankel was crowned the world's best racehorse, with the Australian mare Black Caviar in second.

The unbeaten colt had fulfilled the heavy expectation of his two-year-old season in his Classic year and there was a weight of hope that there was more to come as he developed and matured during the winter months.

Frankel began cantering at the end of January after spending much of the winter trotting in the covered ride at Warren Place. Sir Henry Cecil said: 'Everything is okay with Frankel, who seems to have strengthened over the winter and is shiny in his coat.'

The possibility of a clash with Black Caviar later in the year was mooted in the spring, but Khalid Abdulla's racing manager Teddy Grimthorpe said: 'It's a nice thing to talk about but it's pure speculation at present.'

The build-up continued throughout the spring, with the JLT Lockinge Stakes at Newbury over a mile in May earmarked as Frankel's starting point for a season which was increasingly likely to include a step up to a mile and a quarter. His final race was set for another trip to Champions Day at Ascot and not the Breeders' Cup, with connections all but ruling out a swansong at Santa Anita in California.

As the turf Flat season began at the end of March, Cecil made plans to take Frankel for an overnight stay and gallop at Newbury's Greenham Stakes meeting in the middle of April. It would provide Frankel with his first taste of grass that year, because the dry spell at Newmarket had restricted him to artificial surfaces on the Heath.

However, a week before that planned racecourse gallop Frankel made front-page news for very different reasons after injuring himself on the gallops.

FRANKEL

Opposite: *Work morning:
Frankel, left, on the gallops
(top), and Sir Henry Cecil talks
to Shane Fetherstonhaugh*

*The injury to Frankel's off-fore was described as
superficial, with Grimthorpe saying: 'It probably happened
during work on Racecourse Side yesterday.*

*'I think with a horse like this everything is a concern,
but at the moment it looks superficial and he'll be
monitored and continually checked, and we'll see how
he goes over the next couple of days.*

*'Obviously as time goes on we'll see, but hopefully we'll
get him back moving next week. We hope it's minor and up
until now he's been injury clear.'*

*The first scan was unclear so Frankel was sent for a
second one, and Grimthorpe revealed that Frankel would
probably miss a week's work and connections would wait
until he was ready to return.*

*On Grand National day the Frankel camp were forced to
deny rumours of his retirement.* **Andrew Scutts** *reported:*

Connections of Frankel were last night forced to deny
rumours the unbeaten superstar had been retired in
the wake of the injury to his off-fore he sustained last
Wednesday.

Less than an hour after owner/breeder Khalid Abdulla's
racing manager Teddy Grimthorpe had told the *Racing Post*
there was no change in Frankel's condition, Aintree and
Twitter were alive with rumours to the contrary.

Grimthorpe, who was at Aintree, subsequently went on
Racing UK to clarify that next week's scan – 'towards the
end of the week', as he had earlier told the *Racing Post* –
remains crucial in determining whether Frankel can race
as a four-year-old.

Frankel sustained his injury, which could end his stellar
career if scans reveal tendon damage, while working on
Racecourse Side and trainer Sir Henry Cecil has reasoned
that his exuberant action might have caused his hind leg
to bang the back of his front leg.

Grimthorpe told the *Racing Post*: 'Frankel was led out
this morning, not ridden out. We remain hopeful but the
scan next week will reveal a fuller picture.'

Frankel was due to have a gallop at Newbury next
weekend but Grimthorpe does not believe that will
happen regardless of the scan result, and his scheduled
reappearance in the JLT Lockinge Stakes is reckoned
'very unlikely'.

After the gallop, Teddy Grimthorpe with Sir Henry Cecil

A week later racing got the news it wanted when Frankel was given the green light to resume his normal training routine after the second scan of his off-fore tendon showed no evidence of damage.

A relieved Cecil said: 'I was always very hopeful as it didn't feel like a normal tendon [injury] but you never know. I'd like to make Newbury if possible because it's a long time with a horse like that to hang around until Royal Ascot. I'll feel my way but I'm hopeful.

'He's been going out each morning and each night and he'll probably resume cantering this weekend. It was a bit

of a worry and the prince has been fantastic. He told me, "I've had so much fun out of the horse, he's done more than I ever expected, so don't worry." And I said, "Well, I am worrying, because I think he could be a better horse this year and we need him."'

Grimthorpe added: 'To say that Prince Khalid was elated by the scan result would be an understatement.'

Frankel missed his planned trip to Newbury and instead racegoers at Newmarket on Qipco 2,000 Guineas day were given a treat as Cecil chose that day for his racecourse gallop.

He worked in terrific fashion before racing and Cecil said afterwards: 'He enjoyed that and was relaxed going down, which is good as he wasn't last year. He did everything right.

'Tom [Queally] asked him to go in the last two furlongs and he then had a good blow. He will have another two or three bits of work and so long as it is decent ground he will then run in the Lockinge.'

He was seemingly over his setback and back to his best. He appeared more than ready for his Newbury reappearance in the middle of May.

After the Lockinge, **Lee Mottershead** reported the communal sense of relief.

We can all now breathe a little easier. Just a handful of weeks ago we faced up to the possibility that Frankel's racing days were over. Even when it was announced that retirement was for the future, we feared the damage might have been done.

Reassurance was needed and yesterday in the JLT Lockinge Stakes at Newbury it was given, as the defining horse of our times delivered a stirring reminder of why he very much remains the finest thoroughbred in the world.

At Newmarket on Qipco 2,000 Guineas day there was the racecourse gallop that offered hope. To fix your gaze on him that afternoon was to see a beast even more magnificent than before, every bit as beautiful but beefed up and with greater presence.

In the workout he was flawless, but it was a fake race that ultimately counted for nothing. And yet in its execution, this JLT Lockinge Stakes was almost a carbon copy of what we had witnessed at Newmarket. This was simplicity itself.

As in that racecourse gallop, Frankel sat in the slip-stream of his sibling Bullet Train, enthusiastic and keen but far from unmanageable.

Once again he ranged alongside his stablemate with two furlongs to cover and then, with a surge of acceleration that gladdened his flag-waving fans, stormed clear under Tom Queally, hands and heels driving all that was needed.

At the line five lengths separated him from Excelebration, this time racing for Ballydoyle, still brilliant but still palpably inferior to Khalid Abdulla's supreme champion. Dubawi Gold ran on into third.

'It was very nice,' said Sir Henry Cecil, delivering a perfect definition of understatement before referring us to the April leg injury that sent a shiver down countless spines.

'Getting him back hasn't been straightforward,' explained Cecil. 'When you get a ten-day hiccup before a race it's not very funny. We've had to feel our way and get him here without flattening him out. You can't make up time and just work a horse harder because nature says you have to stop.'

Cecil duly stopped and gave Frankel the rest that was needed. The Lockinge had always been the contest earmarked as the vehicle for his tenth consecutive victory and the date was fulfilled.

Galileo's greatest son, sent off 2-7 favourite, is now the winner of six Group 1 races. The next should be annexed in the Queen Anne Stakes, but where Frankel heads after that, and when he steps up in trip, remains uncertain.

'He's quickened really well and done it very easily,' said Cecil. 'Queally said his acceleration was incredible but he needed the race. His first race is never his best but he had to have a run somewhere before Ascot.

'He's had a good blow and looking back at his last two seasons I'm absolutely certain he'll come on quite a lot for the race.

'All being well, he'll probably tackle a mile and a quarter as the season goes on but there's no hurry. What are we trying to prove? He's in both races at Ascot. I'd say it's more likely he'll go for the Queen Anne, but whether we then go for the Eclipse, the Sussex, the Juddmonte, we'll just see. He will tell me.'

In front of 14,000 racegoers – 3,000 up on last year – Frankel told Queally plenty.

'It's a great privilege,' said the jockey. 'I looked at Excelebration at the start and he looked a million dollars. To kick in with the turbo and go away from a horse like that is amazing. I just have to steer him.

'He's better than everything else in the world. He's head and shoulders above the rest. We're very, very lucky to have him.'

And how much the masters of Coolmore would love him. Aidan O'Brien, who last year saw so many of his best horses humbled by Frankel, was once again left in a state of shock and awe. Excelebration knows the feeling.

'All credit to Frankel,' said O'Brien. 'He's a great horse. Perhaps we should take him on next time with a team of ten and add two fences.'

Then he congratulated the winning connections, repeating the word 'unbelievable', first to Abdulla, then to the owner's racing manager Teddy Grimthorpe and then to Cecil, who at least offered to share the joy around.

'Would you like him?' he asked O'Brien. 'The change would probably do him good.'

Frankel, however, will stay where he is. 'It is exciting and it's lovely for racing,' said Cecil, adding: 'Thank goodness he came through that all right.'

Like Cecil, we all went to bed that little bit happier.

The Lockinge Stakes: Frankel shows he is none the worse for his recent injury

Alastair Down *again:*

Carrying not just Tom Queally but the hopes of a whole Flat season, Frankel purred home by a barely bothered five lengths in yesterday's Lockinge and it is hard to envisage anything being able to lay a glove on him over a mile in the months to come.

Frankel's sheer class and thumping superiority over a field he was entitled to pick up and carry meant that the race lacked drama, but there would have to be something impossible to please about anyone who ever tired of watching this colt in action. He is remorseless, and as he has got older there is an increasingly businesslike air to him, and he ambled round the paddock like a horse for whom the preamble no longer has any perils attached.

In the race he tracked pacemaker Bullet Train, who went half a yard slower than you might have expected, and you knew the race was over even before Queally made his move because you could see his pursuers start to niggle and race while he was hard on the steel.

He led two out and simply oozed clear without being asked any sort of serious question and the winning margin

Frankel returns to the winner's enclosure at Newbury

could easily have been extended, though on his first run of a long season there was no point.

What was interesting afterwards was just how adamant Henry Cecil was in saying he would be better for the run, citing the fact that Frankel had always improved for his first outing of the season and pointing that the colt had 'a very good blow afterwards'.

Queally, who retains a degree of circumspection when dealing with the media, said: 'He's not like anything else I have ever sat on or will ever sit on. He's a handful but that's part of him.'

Cecil, whom the crowd cheered even more ardently round the winner's enclosure than Frankel, was also at pains to stress that Frankel's recent injury problem had genuinely complicated his preparation. He said: 'A ten- to 12-day hiccup wasn't funny. You can't make up for lost time by working them harder and harder. I thought he behaved beautifully today and he is definitely stronger.'

By the sound of it we will next see Frankel in the one-mile Queen Anne Stakes, which kicks off Royal Ascot's opening day, and there is nothing that is going to rattle this colt's cage over eight furlongs.

The big challenge will come when he steps up to a mile and a quarter and that observation has nothing with his getting the trip. You cannot see him having any problem staying ten furlongs and the fact that he races increasingly amenably these days can only help.

It is likely that he will run in York's Juddmonte International in August, a race long sponsored by his owner. We know that nothing can live with Frankel over a mile but going up in distance enfranchises a whole new set of top-class colts, and that could well include some from this year's Classic crop.

Different rivals and a first try at the trip will represent a fresh test. And who knows what Ballydoyle may have to throw at him by then? They rightly tried everything to get Sea The Stars beat and sheer professional pride will ensure they do the same on the Frankel front.

Overall yesterday engendered a sense of relief rather than unbridled excitement. We all have so much riding on this horse and to have him back on track and going very much full steam ahead was all we needed.

In terms of his final place in posterity Frankel is going to have to do something new in order to haul himself higher in the ratings and hopefully he will. He has now beaten the admirable Excelebration four times but that no longer tells us anything new.

But beating the very best Aidan O'Brien mile-and-a-quarter horses over the summer and ace gelding Cirrus Des Aigles and others in a Champion Stakes would write a very different climactic chapter.

And it was striking yesterday how Cecil stressed there was more to come from this horse – the faith Henry has in him is the sort that moves mountains.

The crowd at Newbury was up by 3,000 to 14,000 and, while the place was busy and buzzy, it is actually a slightly disappointing number given that this might be one of the three or four best horses of all time. Why don't Flat superstars pack out courses in quite the same way as the jumping greats?

So now we roll on to Royal Ascot, where they might open up the throttles on the horse to get that great meeting off to a flyer.

Straighter for the run, stronger this season and more mentally composed, there is no reason why Frankel cannot annexe new territories as we all want him to.

And hopefully whoever writes the Qipco Champions series signs, patronisingly paraded in the paddock these days with each horse's name and colours as if the public are all morons, will raise his game. Yesterday the best horse in the world was Frankel. One too many L's for one hell of a horse.

THE RESULT

£99,242 (£37,625; £18,830; £9,380; £4,707; £2,362) **Stalls** Centre

Form						RPR
111-	**1**		**Frankel**[217] 6860 4-9-0 136.. TomQueally 6			139+
			(Sir Henry Cecil) *lw: racd keenly trcking ldr tl led 2f out: sn qcknd: surged clr fnl f: easily*		**2/7**[1]	
12-1	**2**	5	**Excelebration (IRE)**[27] 1549 4-9-0 126............................... JPO'Brien 7			127
			(A P O'Brien, Ire) *disp 3rd tl drvn and qcknd to go 2nd appr fnl f: kpt on wl but nvr any ch w easy wnr*		**10/3**[2]	
4-04	**3**	4	**Dubawi Gold**[22] 1646 4-9-0 117................................... RichardHughes 2			119
			(Richard Hannon) *stdd s and hld up in rr: drvn and qcknd fr 2f out to take 3rd jst ins fnl f but no ch w ldng duo*		**16/1**[3]	
/00-	**4**	3	**Bullet Train**[217] 6860 5-9-0 106................................... IanMongan 5			111
			(Sir Henry Cecil) *led tl hdd 2f out: lost 2nd and fdd appr fnl f*		**100/1**	
00-0	**5**	7	**Ransom Note**[30] 1471 5-9-0 115................................... KierenFallon 3			95
			(Charles Hills) *disp 3rd: rdn over 3f out: btn over 2f out*		**33/1**	
-031	**6**	2 ¼	**Windsor Palace (IRE)**[12] 1946 7-9-0 104.............(v[1]) SeamieHeffernan 4			90
			(A P O'Brien, Ire) *disp 3rd and pushed along 4f out: wknd wl over 2f out*		**40/1**	

1m 38.1s (-1.56) **Going Correction** +0.325s/f (Good)   **6** Ran   SP% **113.1**
Speed ratings (Par 117): **120,115,111,108,101 98**
toteswingers: 1&2 £1.10, 1&3 £1.60, 2&3 £1.50 CSF £1.59 TOTE £1.40: £1.02, £1.70; EX 1.80.
Owner K Abdulla **Bred** Juddmonte Farms Ltd **Trained** Newmarket, Suffolk

Analysis

GRAHAM DENCH

With two pacemakers in a field of six and 33-1 chance Ransom Note the only new face among the others this was a straightforward task for Frankel on his reappearance, but it was not entirely routine as he had missed work following his career-threatening tendon injury and this was our first sight of him since.

All went smoothly and his domination was total once again as he quickened away in the last two furlongs, having sat in Bullet Train's slipstream from the start. He looked as good as ever in extending his superiority over old rivals Excelebration, now with Aidan O'Brien, and Dubawi Gold to five lengths and nine lengths respectively.

RACECARD

2.30 — RACE 1 — **BBC1**

Queen Anne Stakes (British Champions Series) (Group 1) (Class 1)
Winner £198,485 — 1m Str

£350,000 guaranteed **For** 4yo+ **Weights** colts and geldings 9st; fillies 8st 11lb **Allowances** southern hemisphere: 4yo 1lb **Entries** 34 pay £1200 **1st Forfeit** 19 pay £1400 **Confirmed** 12 pay £900 **Penalty value 1st** £198,485 **2nd** £75,250 **3rd** £37,660 **4th** £18,760 **5th** £9,415 **6th** £4,725 **Tariff** £160,000

1 (6) — 55/78-4 **BULLET TRAIN** [31] **D1** — b h Sadler's Wells-Kind — Sir Henry Cecil — K Abdulla — Ian Mongan — 5 9-0 — (125)

2 (3) — 3112-12 **EXCELEBRATION** (IRE) (TTF)[31] **D2** — b c Exceed And Excel-Sun Shower — A P O'Brien (IRE) — D Smith, Mrs J Magnier, M Tabor — J P O'Brien — 4 9-0 — (143)

3 (8) — 11111-1 **FRANKEL** (TTF)[31] **D6 C2 CD1** — b c Galileo-Kind — Sir Henry Cecil — K Abdulla — Tom Queally — 4 9-0 — (153)

4 (10) — 17375-2 **INDOMITO** (GER) [65] — b h Areion-Insola — A Wohler (GER) — Stall 5-Stars — William Buick — 6 9-0 — (124)

5 (11) — 5127-11 **PREMIO LOCO** (USA) (TTF)[35] **D9 C1** — ch g Prized-Crazee Mental — Chris Wall — Bernard Westley — George Baker — 8 9-0 — (127)

6 (4) — 542-314 **RED JAZZ** (USA) (TTF)[17] **BF C1** — b h Johannesburg-Now That's Jazz — Charles Hills — R J Arculli — Michael Hills — 5 9-0 — (130)

7 (5) — 147-531 **SIDE GLANCE** (TTF)[18] **D3 C1 CD1** — br g Passing Glance-Averami — Andrew Balding — Qatar Racing Limited — Jimmy Fortune — 5 9-0 — (130)

8 (1) — 613110- **STRONG SUIT** (USA) (TTF)[227] **C2** — ch c Rahy-Helwa — Richard Hannon — Qatar Racing Limited — Richard Hughes — 4 9-0 — (140)

9 (7) — 55-0316 **WINDSOR PALACE** (IRE) [31] **D1** — b h Danehill Dancer-Simaat — A P O'Brien (IRE) — D Smith, Mrs J Magnier, M Tabor — Seamie Heffernan — v 7 9-0 — (121)

10 (2) — 2195-14 **WORTHADD** (IRE) [18] **BF D5** — b h Dubawi-Wigman — Sir Mark Prescott Bt — Diego Romeo — Frankie Dettori — 5 9-0 — (130)

11 (9) — 118-500 **HELMET** (AUS) (TTF)[80] **D2** — ch c Exceed And Excel-Accessories — Mahmood Al Zarooni[1] — Godolphin — Mickael Barzalona — tp 4 8-13 — (134)

2011 (7 ran) Canford Cliffs (6) Richard Hannon 4 9-0 11/8 — Richard Hughes RPR130

BETTING FORECAST: 1-6 Frankel, 6 Excelebration, 10 Strong Suit, 33 Helmet, Side Glance, Worthadd, 50 Premio Loco, Red Jazz, 66 Indomito, 200 Bullet Train, Windsor Palace.

Queen Anne Stakes

Royal Ascot, June 19, 2012

Frankel's performance in the Lockinge Stakes was worthy of at least a reproduction of his best Racing Post Rating of 139+, according to Paul Curtis, who wrote: 'On paper this could rate Frankel's best performance, having given Excelebration and Dubawi Gold a slightly bigger beating than in the Queen Elizabeth II Stakes in October. But given the early stage of the season and an interrupted preparation to this reappearance, confirmation of his brilliance was perhaps as much as could have been hoped for.

'While plenty went Frankel's way he again left the strong impression we've yet to see the very best of him. To produce such a figure first time up would seem to back the view. The highest-rated turf horse in RPR history and joint-top overall with Dubai Millennium, it will be a surprise if Frankel doesn't stand alone by the end of the year.'

Hopes of a clash between Frankel and unbeaten Australian supermare Black Caviar were again raised, but those were dashed when the Australian camp said she would not be entered for the Sussex Stakes, which would be Frankel's next start but one following the Queen Anne Stakes at Royal Ascot.

Following the scintillating success of Camelot in the Derby at Epsom, when he followed up his triumph in the 2,000 Guineas, Cecil said he was excited about the possibility of the dual Classic hero meeting with Frankel.

'Hopefully Camelot will go for the Juddmonte and I would love it because it would be exciting,' he said.

Cecil said he expected Frankel to improve for that outing. 'I am not saying he is going to be but he could be 3lb or 4lb better,' he said.

'I think he is better, he is stronger this year. I didn't push him but I have never pushed him for his first race anyway, as a two-year-old, a three-year-old or four-year-old. Like a lot of trainers we don't have them 100 per cent first time out. That is just the beginning of the season.'

Looking toward the rest of the campaign, Cecil added: 'Frankel has got important engagements as the season goes on and the main thing is as long as he can win, let's hope he can win well, it does not matter if it is by two lengths or ten lengths.

'The Juddmonte will be the most interesting as he is going another two and half furlongs and he is going against different horses.'

Frankel was set to start as one of the shortest-priced Royal Ascot favourites of modern times as connections reported that he had continued to work nicely in the days before the Queen Anne Stakes. The royal meeting wasn't all about Frankel, though, as Black Caviar would be making her British debut in the Diamond Jubilee Stakes on the final day. However, all eyes were on the world's best racehorse on the opening day – Tuesday – and he did not disappoint, extending his unbeaten record with an astonishing 11-length success. The following morning the Racing Post *splashed with, 'INCREDIBLE – The world's best just got even better' – and* **Jon Lees** *was there to record an electrifying performance.*

There were two royal processions at Ascot yesterday. One for the Queen, the other for a king.

Yet while the arrival of the reigning monarch by carriage is a daily Royal Ascot highlight, Frankel's appearance will be remembered for many, many years after the world's best racehorse delivered a defining performance in the Queen Anne Stakes.

In the race retained as the first of three Group 1s to provide an explosive start to the meeting, Frankel duly delivered the pyrotechnics, spreadeagling ten rivals to hand out the rout of all routs.

He increased his margin of supremacy over Excelebration by more than double the five lengths he had managed in three previous meetings, easing to the front two furlongs out and stretching away to record his 11th straight victory by a staggering 11 lengths in a time of 1min 37.85 seconds – 0.69 second outside the race record on good to soft ground.

Frankel was well into a lap of the round course before jockey Tom Queally could pull him up. The best is getting better.

'It was lovely,' said trainer Sir Henry Cecil. 'He could not have done any more. He's improving.

Frankel destroys his rivals in the Queen Anne Stakes

'It's fantastic that [owner-breeder] Prince Khalid should keep him on and I'm very lucky to be training him. He takes some pulling up. He will definitely get a mile and a quarter.

'You have to unleash Frankel in good time and then gallop the others into the ground. He's got that long stride and I wanted him produced between two and two and a half furlongs out because he takes some catching. He keeps going when others don't.

'I've been fortunate to have trained a lot of good horses like Wollow, Bolkonski, Bosra Sham and Kris and I have my view where they would have finished in a race together, but people can decide for themselves.'

He continued: 'Black Caviar and Frankel are both exceptional champions in their own right over different distances. You can't compare them and it makes no sense to race one against another.

'It would have been very sad if he had got beaten today. It's like supporting a football team. It's important people

Tom Queally shows his delight after the race

have something to get involved in. People not really in the racing world have latched on to him.

'Like great sportsmen, like Tiger Woods or [Andy] Murray, it's important to have something to watch, admire and support. Thanks to all the public.'

Frankel's second visit to Royal Ascot was much more satisfying than a year ago, when the idling colt was almost caught late on in the St James's Palace Stakes.

Queally said: 'He's been flawless in the past but I couldn't ask for any more today. It was a demolition again – he was awesome. This year everyone has latched on and grasped what it's all about. He was very, very good.

'We had a plan to go on when we did and it worked perfectly. It didn't surprise me that he won so far because he felt so good. I pinch myself every morning having a horse like this to ride, so of course I'm looking forward to the challenges ahead.'

Those challenges could involve the Coral-Eclipse, for which he is 1-5 with a run with the sponsor, the Qipco Sussex Stakes, Juddmonte International and Qipco

He was just breathtaking. He just kept going further away. It was his best performance since the Guineas.

It's great for the public that he's so spectacular. People love a good horse and it's important for the sport.

I said last year he was the best horse I have ever seen and I still think he is.

He's certainly the best miler I've seen and it will be very exciting for racing to see him step up to a mile and a quarter.

Frankel is a great horse, the greatest miler I have seen. I have been around a long time, you know, and for the very best horse I would have to say Sea-Bird.

He's not the biggest horse but he's a giant when he gets on the track, he has got such a stride on him. It's a pity he won't be racing against Black Caviar, who wins her races in the same way as him.

Champion or Queen Elizabeth II Stakes, but Cecil would not commit himself.

'There is a chance he will take another four races but we will see,' said the trainer.

'It's a question of how he takes the races. If he is jumping out of his skin we'll consider the Eclipse, otherwise we will wait for the Sussex and go for the Juddmonte. We'll feel our way but it will be the prince's decision.'

Khalid Abdulla was in Saudi Arabia attending the funeral of Crown Prince Nayef but his manager, Teddy Grimthorpe, said: 'Frankel was breathtaking. It was controlled brilliance.

'Everything went smoothly, he accelerated and showed a beautiful action.'

BetVictor do not believe Frankel will be beaten this season and have decided to pay out those who had backed him to continue his winning streak throughout 2012.

Alastair Down *was bowled over by the occasion.*

We are all on some extraordinary ride into realms hitherto untapped with Frankel. At an enraptured Ascot yesterday, he continued to redefine our notion of what a racehorse is capable of achieving with a performance in the Queen Anne that was almost shocking for the contempt with which he fed a top-class field mercilessly through the mangle.

Have no doubt that this colt means we are living in wondrous times, perhaps not seen before and, for all we know, the likes of which may not come again.

Hours after this victory, by 11 shiver-inducing lengths if you please, Timeform provisionally awarded Frankel the highest rating in their 64-year history – putting him on 147, two clear of the Swinging Sixties superstar Sea-Bird and three ahead of Brigadier Gerard and Tudor Minstrel. We are in oxygen territory here – stratospheres come no more rarefied.

Timeform is not a deity, its judges no finer than the *Racing Post*'s young lions, but its longevity as observer bestows on it a degree of authority. It has been keeper of the flames of great superstars past; now it has seen something utterly new that has swept the old order away.

There is a popular belief that the great horses, high-mettled creatures of class and impeccable pedigree, are things of palpable beauty, all flow and finesse. And while that can indeed be true it is not the way with Frankel.

There is something earthier and almost primeval about him and every stride roars power – the power to destroy.

There is much that is magical or magnificent about this horse, but pretty he isn't. Images of Frankel should never adorn the tops of chocolate boxes or biscuit tins; they belong carved exquisitely on to the butts of a 12-bore, as there is something about his overwhelming brilliance that has the whiff of danger, menace even.

Tom Queally took him steadier than ever down to post yesterday, through the last couple of minutes prior to the volcano's eruption.

And if you want beauty then it lies in the blitzkrieg Frankel can produce when all the tonnage of the beast is unleashed. He took it up just over two furlongs out and that is where the awe cut in.

At some stage just after Frankel had hit the front you could almost sense Queally gritting his teeth and saying: 'Go on son, go and show 'em what you are made of.' The rest, that last furlong and a half of Berkshire turf, was suddenly the stuff of racing history as he barrelled his barnstorming way clear to win by a breadth of daylight that made you question your ideas of the feasible.

People keep asking Frankel to do something more, something different, something new. God save and spare us as we must be a mighty hard-to-please generation.

This time, instead of beating old foe Excelebration by his customary four or five lengths, Frankel pulverised him by a take-no-prisoners 11. There was more than a hint of exasperation in Queally's voice when he half-joked: 'What more do you want? If he was any better I'd be pulling him up in Legoland.'

And sometimes it is in the tiny snapshot that you suddenly see the bigger picture. Among the very first people rooted by the rail round Ascot's new inner winner's enclosure were two training legends who you might imagine had seen it all but were damned if they were going to miss a seat ringside for the return of this changer of the racing weather.

They answer, usually with a one-liner, to the names of Peter Easterby and Mick O'Toole, each a giant under both codes and bringing to the party more than 160 years of savvy. Yet there they were at the front of the queue struck, like a couple of schoolkids, by the might of the moment and the imminent thrill of proximity to the extraordinary.

Frankel with connections in the winner's enclosure

And then Frankel returned to a real roar. You can keep your polite applause for the croquet lawn or the village fete dog show – this was the throat-opening stuff of real acclaim.

And gliding round his charge was the old headmaster who probably never, ever, in the highest-flown flight of his imagination, thought he would have a pupil like this one at his Warren Place academy. Sir Henry Cecil had butterflies on his tie, presumably chosen to keep the ones in his tummy company pre-race.

With a fencer's skill he parried press thrusts for exact plans for Frankel. Henry doesn't strike me as enamoured with Sandown for Frankel's first foray over ten furlongs, but he will most certainly be there at York for the Juddmonte in August.

After the manner of yesterday's triumph it may be that few will want to take him on, but there are surely enough folk among the top owners who will want to give it a charge in a race in which the act of God that was Derby winner Roberto inflicted Brigadier Gerard's sole defeat.

We will see Frankel three, maybe four times again, so I repeat my plea to anyone whose life has ever been illuminated by a racehorse to move heaven and earth to go to see him.

Just the other day folk were getting excited about the passage of Venus across the sun because it won't happen again until December 2117.

Believe me, we could have had another dozen passages of Venus before we get another Frankel. One happens rarely, this one is really happening.

In the Racing Post, *Topspeed echoed the line about two royal processions.*

There is a daily procession at Royal Ascot but on this occasion there were two in quick succession as Frankel nonchalantly brushed aside his rivals. More pliant and tractable as a four-year-old, Sir Henry Cecil's ace covered the first half of the race in 50.96 and then upped his game to clock 11.26, and a lung-bursting 10.58. He hit 42.53mph and no runner in the King's Stand the same afternoon could match his searing sixth-furlong split.

After five furlongs he held a narrow three-hundredths of a second advantage over smart Excelebration but during the sixth and seventh furlongs he took a staggering 1.18 seconds out of the high-class second and even though he eased off in the final furlong he took a further 0.69 seconds out of him. In short he ripped the best part of two seconds out of a multiple Group 1 winner in the final three furlongs.

It was another case of him producing Group 1 sprinter's pace for three-eighths of the race and it is that rare ability to sustain such devastating pace for a relatively long period that makes him peerless.

THE RESULT

3237   **QUEEN ANNE STKS (BRITISH CHAMPIONS SERIES) (GROUP 1)**   **1m (S)**
2:30 (2:34) (Class 1) 4-Y-O+

£198,485 (£75,250; £37,660; £18,760; £9,415; £4,725) **Stalls** Centre

Form							RPR
11-1	**1**		**Frankel**[31] 2270 4-9-0 138... TomQueally 8				142+

11-1   **1**   **Frankel**[31] 2270 4-9-0 138.. TomQueally 8   142+
(Sir Henry Cecil) *lw: trckd ldrs a gng wl: led over 2f out: shkn up over 1f out: sn qcknd clr: edgd sltly rt ins fnl f: extremely impressive*   **1/10**[1]

2-12   **2**   11   **Excelebration (IRE)**[31] 2270 4-9-0 125.............................. JPO'Brien 3   117
(A P O'Brien, Ire) *a.p: wnt 2nd over 2f out: rdn and unable to go w wnr over 1f out: no ch fnl f: all out to hold on for 2nd*   **5/1**[2]

-531   **3**   nk   **Side Glance**[18] 2656 5-9-0 113.. JimmyFortune 5   116
(Andrew Balding) *racd keenly in tch: effrt over 2f out: wnt 3rd over 1f out: styd on towards fin: pressed 2nd cl home*   **33/1**

05-2   **4**   1   **Indomito (GER)**[65] 1410 6-9-0 108.............................. WilliamBuick 10   113
(A Wohler, Germany) *hld up: swtchd rt over 2f out: rdn and hdwy over 1f out: styd on towards fin: nvr able to chal*   **50/1**

0316   **5**   3   **Windsor Palace (IRE)**[31] 2270 7-9-0 104.............(v) SeamieHeffernan 7   106
(A P O'Brien, Ire) *s.i.s: racd in rr div and niggled along most of way: prog ins fnl f: styd on: nvr gng pce to get competitive*   **100/1**

00-4   **6**   ³⁄₄   **Bullet Train**[31] 2270 5-9-0 111... IanMongan 6   105
(Sir Henry Cecil) *led: pushed along and hdd over 2f out: sn outpcd: no ch fnl f*   **66/1**

0-0   **7**   nk   **Helmet (AUS)**[80] 1145 4-8-13 119........................(tp) MickaelBarzalona 9   103
(Mahmood Al Zarooni) *racd keenly: prom: pushed along 3f out: outpcd ent fnl 2f: no ch fnl f*   **20/1**

0-11   **8**   1 ¹⁄₂   **Premio Loco (USA)**[35] 2160 8-9-0 113.......................... GeorgeBaker 11   101
(Chris Wall) *midfield: pushed along over 2f out: sn outpcd: no imp after*   **50/1**

-314   **9**   ³⁄₄   **Red Jazz (USA)**[17] 2710 5-9-0 112.................................... MichaelHills 4   99
(Charles Hills) *hld up in midfield: pushed along 3f out: wl btn over 1f out*   **50/1**

110-   **10**   ¹⁄₂   **Strong Suit (USA)**[227] 7307 4-9-0 123......................... RichardHughes 1   98
(Richard Hannon) *lw: stdd early on: hld up: effrt in midfield over 1f out: no imp: sn wknd*   **10/1**[3]

5-14   **11**   1 ¹⁄₂   **Worthadd (IRE)**[18] 2656 5-9-0 118................................ FrankieDettori 2   94
(Sir Mark Prescott Bt) *lw: handy: rdn 2f out: wknd over 1f out*   **20/1**

1m 37.8s (-2.95) **Going Correction** +0.175s/f (Good) course record **11** Ran   SP% **137.5**
Speed ratings (Par 117): **121,110,109,108,105** 104,104,103,102,101 **100**
toteswingers:1&2:£1.10, 2&3:£11.50, 1&3:£6.10 CSF £1.78 CT £16.79 TOTE £1.10: £1.10, £1.30, £5.50; EX 1.90 Trifecta £15.10 Pool: £37438.42 - 1824.51 winning units..
Owner K Abdulla **Bred** Juddmonte Farms Ltd **Trained** Newmarket, Suffolk

Analysis

GRAHAM DENCH

The first race of the meeting and a performance to exceed even the wildest expectations as Frankel extended his unbeaten run to 11 races with an 11-length annihilation of old rival Excelebration, tanking his way to the front with more than two furlongs to go and registering a faster final furlong than any of the sprint specialists in the later King's Stand Stakes.

It was an extraordinary performance, even by Frankel's extraordinary standards, and one that confirmed he was still improving. His Racing Post Rating was elevated another 3lb to a record 142.

3.10 RACE 3

Qipco Sussex Stakes (British Champions Series) (Group 1) (Class 1)

CH4

Winner £179,487.15

1m

£300,000 guaranteed **For** 3yo+ **Weights** 3yo colts and geldings 9st; fillies 8st 11lb; 4yo+ colts and geldings 9st 7lb; fillies 9st 4lb **Weight for age** 3 from 4yo+ 7lb **Entries** 37 pay £1000 **1st Forfeit** 17 pay £1500 **2nd Forfeit** 1 pay £19500 **Confirmed** 8 pay £500 **Penalty value 1st** £179,487.15 **2nd** £68,047.50 **3rd** £34,055.40 **4th** £16,964.40 **Tariff** £160,000

1 (2)	5/78-46 **BULLET TRAIN** [43] **D1** b h Sadler's Wells-Kind **Sir Henry Cecil** K Abdulla	5 9-7 Ian Mongan (118)	
2 (4)	1/1-132 **FARHH** [25] **BF D2** b c Pivotal-Gonbarda **Saeed Bin Suroor** Godolphin	4 9-7 Frankie Dettori (135)	
3 (3)	1111-11 **FRANKEL** (TTF)[43] **D7 CD1** b c Galileo-Kind **Sir Henry Cecil** K Abdulla	4 9-7 Tom Queally (149)	
4 (1)	10-7215 **GABRIAL** (IRE) [43] **D1** b c Dark Angel-Guajira **Richard Fahey** Dr Marwan Koukash	3 9-0 Paul Hanagan (117)	

2011 (4 ran) Frankel (3) Sir Henry Cecil 3 8-13 8/13F   Tom Queally RPR137

BETTING FORECAST: 1-16 Frankel, 10 Farhh, 50 Gabrial, 100 Bullet Train.

Qipco Sussex Stakes

Goodwood, August 1, 2012

Frankel became the first horse to break the glass ceiling mark of 140 with a new Racing Post Rating of 142 for his Royal Ascot romp. The decision to keep him in training had undoubtedly helped him in this regard because he had clearly developed from three to four, with more progress expected.

Phil Smith, head of handicapping at the British Horseracing Authority, believed that Frankel could reach Dancing Brave's all-time official highest rating of 141. Dancing Brave, although top rated, only leads the ratings in the modern era. Smith said of the Queen Anne Stakes victory: 'It was the most visually stunning performance I've seen in 40 years of rating horses. He effortlessly tanked to the front before powering clear for what was his most impressive performance in terms of form anyway.'

During the race Frankel lost a shoe and Sir Henry Cecil reported the next day that the colt was none the worse for the experience and his right foreleg was in poultice as a precaution. The shoe was recovered after the race and became an auction lot at the 2012 Sir Peter O'Sullevan Trust annual charity lunch.

A defence of his Sussex Stakes title was next on the agenda for Frankel, and after starting at 1-10 at Royal Ascot, it was predicted that he could start as short as 1-20 at Glorious Goodwood as the opposition melted away. Petite Etoile, who scored at 1-10 in 1959, was the shortest-priced winner of the Sussex Stakes since the war – before Frankel.

Sir Henry Cecil had been present for all of Frankel's races but was absent from Glorious Goodwood because of ongoing treatment for cancer.

On the opening day of the meeting Sir Henry's wife Jane reported her husband to be 'doing well and very positive' as she looked forward to the possibility of Flat racing's most popular trainer being healthy enough to be at York for Frankel's planned assault on the Juddmonte International on August 22.

The Post *splashed with 'ANY TAKERS? Frankel 1-16 for York after Sussex demolition job leaves bookies searching for rivals – on this side of the Channel at least'.*
Lee Mottershead *filed from Goodwood.*

The possibility of Frankel exhibiting his incomparable powers outside Britain for the first time was raised yesterday after racing's wonder horse delivered a performance so stunning that one leading bookmaker now quotes him as short as 1-16 for the Juddmonte International on August 22.

While most had expected the Sussex Stakes to mark Frankel's final outing over a mile and the third-last of his career, a revision of long-held plans will be considered with Longchamp's Prix du Moulin revealed as a fresh option.

Teddy Grimthorpe, racing manager to owner Khalid Abdulla, confirmed Frankel would end his career at Ascot in the Qipco Champion Stakes in October, but the lengthy eight-week gap between the York showpiece and British Champions Day could now prompt Sir Henry Cecil to consider giving the sport's world champion an extra outing.

Running in the Moulin, staged at Longchamp on September 16, would require Frankel to drop back to a mile immediately after his first attempt at a mile and a quarter. But the four-year-old's dominance over his familiar distance was once again evident yesterday as he justified

Frankel mania catches on

One-horse race: the paddock
board at Goodwood

1-20 favouritism and became the first dual Sussex winner
with a typically flawless six-length defeat of Godolphin's
top-class performer Farhh.

As has become habitual, Frankel drifted right in the
closing stages, perhaps offering one minuscule crumb
of hope for opponents when he visits the left-handed
Knavesmire. That trait, however, in no way concerns
connections, while, helpfully for the Warren Place legend,
races at York invariably now unfold centre to stands' side.

'There are two obvious races, the Juddmonte and the
Champion Stakes,' said Grimthorpe. 'It's quite a gap, nearly
two months, between those two races and Henry might
want to give him a race in something like the Moulin in
between. We'll have to think about that.'

What is certain is that Frankel will run next in the
International, a contest sponsored by Abdulla, who was
represented at Goodwood by his son Prince Ahmad.
Bookmakers rate rivals thin on the ground. Coral quote
the 12-time winner – whose seventh consecutive Group 1
triumph equalled Rock Of Gibraltar's record – at 1-16 for
that race, whereas William Hill offer 1-5, the same price
Coral issued about Frankel for the Champion.

'That will have hopefully set him up for York and
it's what Henry was looking for in every way,' added
Grimthorpe. 'I think stepping him up in trip is hugely
exciting. It's a new challenge for him, it's what everybody
wants to see him do and I think the horse is ready to do it.'

Previous spread: *Frankel finishes clear of Farhh, Gabrial and Bullet Train…*

Tom Queally, who took a long look at toiling rivals before sending Frankel past pacemaker Bullet Train just over two furlongs out, said: 'Every moment spent on his back is a special moment and today was no different. He had all the other horses cooked a little after halfway. It was a nice prep for his next race.'

And **Alastair Down** *had his usual individual perspective.*

Yes it was a formality, but a compelling one nonetheless, as the sands of Frankel's racing time are running against us now and where there is currently wonder all too soon it will be memory.

Ever cooler and more collected in the preliminaries, his races have become a question of exactly when Tom Queally chooses to deliver the coup de grace of this horse's change of gear that seems to come from some parallel universe. He doesn't merely beat 'em, he pulverises them.

It is not just that this horse of so many lifetimes is better than anything else around, it is the almost unquantifiable degree of his superiority that makes the awe kick in.

And all the half-lit fuse element of his earlier days has been replaced by a rock-steady demeanour that makes him all the more intimidating because the last chink in his armour has been closed up.

How the team at Warren Place have tamed the tearaway side to Frankel we don't know, but they have done us all an inestimable service.

In Sir Henry Cecil we have one national sporting treasure orchestrating the career of another and if he has put a foot wrong it hasn't been spotted by this observer.

Truth be told this second Sussex Stakes was one of Frankel's more routine assignments. He flogged Farhh six lengths and Queally didn't open the throttle here to the degree he did when powering home by 11 lengths at Ascot as the terrain here is just that touch less straightforward.

Goodwood is no place to run risks as yesterday proved with two fallers and a third horse humanely despatched.

So now the challenge for Frankel is ratcheted up a fraction with the extended ten furlongs of the Knavesmire next on the hit-list in the Juddmonte International, although looking through the 19 horses left in York's great race there is nothing that leaps off the page as a credible threat.

... and returns to a packed winner's enclosure

Mind you, everyone must have said the same when Brigadier Gerard journeyed up the Great North Road to get beat by Roberto and a passing pilot from Panama.

Interestingly, Lord not-at-all Grimthorpe raised the possibility here of Frankel having a run between York on August 22 and the Champion Stakes on October 20, pointing out that two months is a long old gap between races.

The race suggested was the Prix du Moulin over a mile at Longchamp on September 16, but we will see.

Sir Henry may have to apply for a passport as he has never been mad about running horses in France and the last time he crossed the Channel may have been on a trip from school.

Grimthorpe stressed that however brilliant Frankel may be, or undoubtedly is, you can not turn up for a Group 1 off anything other than a searching and thorough preparation. He said: 'You can't come for races like this half-prepared or you could end up looking stupid, so he came here pretty much at the top of his game.'

What Grimthorpe was saying is that all races involve the risk of defeat and that you can't flirt with disaster by leaving even a horse of this epochal magnitude slightly undercooked. There is no complacency about this horse despite his overwhelming superiority.

Yesterday was a golden day of sport in Britain and it was notable that, despite the Olympics, there was a reporter at Goodwood from CNN whose reports from British racecourses can be counted on the fingers of your foot.

The message must be getting through to the wider world at last that we live in interesting times, as the Chinese would say.

Frankel put a couple of thousand on the gate here and all of you who have yet to see the miracle in the flesh have two more chances to see him on home territory. Believe me he must be seen for the simple reason that the likes of him have not trod the turf before and may well never do so again.

The form book says we see the likes of him every 300 years or so. However much you think medical science is likely to increase our lifespan I'd go for it now rather than wait for the next one.

The energetic David Redvers presented the trophy on behalf of Qipco yesterday but before he did so he pushed two youngsters under ten to the front of the winner's enclosure crowd telling them that this was a horse who in their old age they could tell people they had seen when knee-high to a grasshopper.

It may have meant little to them yesterday but in the fullness of time they will understand that they had a ringside glimpse of a big piece of history.

THE RESULT

4699	QIPCO SUSSEX STKS (BRITISH CHAMPIONS SERIES) (GROUP 1)	1m
	3:10 (3:11) (Class 1) 3-Y-O+ £179,487 (£68,047; £34,055; £16,964)	**Stalls** Low

Form					RPR
1-11	**1**		**Frankel**[43] 3237 4-9-7 140.. TomQueally 3		138+
			(Sir Henry Cecil) *travelled strly: sn trcking pcemaker: cruised upsides 3f out: led 2f out: shkn up and readily qcknd clr over 1f out: eased towards fin: v easily*	**1/20**[1]	
-132	**2**	6	**Farhh**[25] 3880 4-9-7 122.. FrankieDettori 4		119
			(Saeed Bin Suroor) *broke wl: sn stdd bk and hld up in 3rd: rdn and sltly outpcd over 3f out: styd on to chse clr wnr over 1f out: no imp and wl hld after*	**11/1**[2]	
0215	**3**	3¼	**Gabrial (IRE)**[43] 3239 3-9-0 108...................................... PaulHanagan 1		110
			(Richard Fahey) *stdd s: t.k.h early: hld up in rr: pushed along and effrt over 3f out: outpcd and wl btn 2f out: kpt on u.p and wnt modest 3rd ins fnl f*	**80/1**[3]	
0-46	**4**	½	**Bullet Train**[43] 3237 5-9-7 111... IanMongan 2		110
			(Sir Henry Cecil) *led: rdn and hdd 2f out: outpcd and immediately brushed aside by wnr over 1f out: lost modest 3rd ins fnl f*	**150/1**	

1m 37.6s (-2.34) **Going Correction** +0.075s/f (Good)
WFA 3 from 4yo+ 7lb   **4** Ran   SP% **105.5**
Speed ratings (Par 117): **114,108,104,104**
CSF £1.11 TOTE £1.10; EX 1.40.
Owner K Abdulla **Bred** Juddmonte Farms Ltd **Trained** Newmarket, Suffolk

Analysis

GRAHAM DENCH

Nothing like the sense of anticipation that preceded the 2011 head-to-head with Canford Cliffs, for Frankel had little to prove against just three rivals, one of whom was now regular pacemaker Bullet Train. The other two were new rivals in Coral-Eclipse second Farhh, whom he had been due to meet at Doncaster at two, and talented three-year-old Gabrial, yet there was still a feeling that it was high time Frankel faced a new challenge.

Though not one of Frankel's most spectacular performances, all went smoothly and he disposed of Farhh and Gabrial as easily as most expected him to. In doing so, he became the first ever dual winner of the Sussex Stakes.

RACECARD

3.40
RACE 4

Juddmonte International Stakes CH4
(British Champions Series) (Group 1)
(Class 1)
Winner £411,147.50   (1m 2f 88y)**1m2¹/₂f**

£725,000 guaranteed **For** 3yo+ **Weights** 3yo colts and geldings 8st 11lb; fillies 8st 8lb; 4yo+ colts and geldings 9st 5lb; fillies 9st 2lb **Entries** 40 pay £2500 **1st Forfeit** 19 pay £2900 **Confirmed** 10 pay £1850 **Penalty value 1st** £411,147.50 **2nd** £155,875 **3rd** £78,010 **4th** £38,860 **5th** £19,502.50 **6th** £9,787.50 **Tariff** £160,000

1 (6)	/78-464	**BULLET TRAIN** [21] *b h Sadler's Wells-Kind* **Sir Henry Cecil** K Abdulla	5 9-5 Eddie Ahern	(120)
2 (4)	/1-1322	●**FARHH** [21] *b c Pivotal-Gonbarda* **Saeed Bin Suroor** Godolphin	4 9-5 Frankie Dettori	(135)
3 (7)	111-111	**FRANKEL** (TTF)[21] *b c Galileo-Kind* **Sir Henry Cecil** K Abdulla	4 9-5 Tom Queally	151
4 (8)	458-337	**PLANTEUR** (IRE) (TTF)[63] **D3** *b h Danehill Dancer-Plante Rare* **Marco Botti** Mohamed Albousi Alghafli	5 9-5 Ryan Moore	(128)
5 (5)	4343600	**ROBIN HOOD** (IRE) [32] **D1** *b c Galileo-Banquise* **A P O'Brien (IRE)** Mrs John Magnier & Michael Tabor & Derrick Smith	v 4 9-5 Seamie Heffernan	(110)
6 (2)	7-16571	**SRI PUTRA** (TTF)[25] **D1** **CD1** *b h Oasis Dream-Wendylina* **Roger Varian** H R H Sultan Ahmad Shah	hb 6 9-5 Neil Callan	(127)
7 (3)	51-2213	**ST NICHOLAS ABBEY** (IRE) (TTF)[32] *b h Montjeu-Leaping Water* **A P O'Brien (IRE)** Derrick Smith & Mrs John Magnier & Michael Tabor	5 9-5 J P O'Brien	(136)
8 (9)	110-233	**TWICE OVER** (TTF)[46] **D7** **CD2** *b/br h Observatory-Double Crossed* **Sir Henry Cecil** K Abdulla	7 9-5 Ian Mongan	(135)
9 (1)	0316545	**WINDSOR PALACE** (IRE) [27] **D1** *br h Danehill Dancer-Simaat* **A P O'Brien (IRE)** Derrick Smith & Mrs John Magnier & Michael Tabor	v 7 9-5 C O'Donoghue	(116)

●**FARHH** runs only if suitable ground, states trainer

2011 (5 ran) **Twice Over** (4) Sir Henry Cecil 6 9-5 11/2   Ian Mongan RPR126

BETTING FORECAST: 1-7 Frankel, 5 St Nicholas Abbey, 12 Farhh, 16 Twice Over, 33 Planteur, 50 Sri Putra, 100 Windsor Palace, 150 Bullet Train, 200 Robin Hood.

Juddmonte
International Stakes

York, August 22, 2012

After the triumphant defence of his Sussex Stakes crown at Goodwood the racecourse management estimated that Frankel had put an extra 5,000 on the attendance figure for the second day of the Glorious meeting.

Sir Henry Cecil described the possibility of Frankel heading to France for the Prix du Moulin as 'questionable', but he would leave it to the colt to indicate if he needed a prep before his expected final appearance on British Champions Day at Ascot.

Cecil added: 'I was delighted with Frankel. He has grown up a lot mentally and took it all like a true professional.

'The idea was to be as easy as we could with him as it was a warm-up to the Juddmonte International. He seems to have come out of yesterday's race really well and is on course for the Knavesmire.'

Frankel's performance at Goodwood was rewarded with a Racing Post Rating of 138+, his fifth consecutive RPR of 137+ since taking on all-aged opposition in the previous year's Sussex Stakes, a sequence completed with a winning margin totalling 31 lengths.

Frankel was now all set to head north for only the second time in his career for his first run over more than a mile in the race sponsored by his owner – the Juddmonte International Stakes at York's popular Ebor festival.

During August, Teddy Grimthorpe was forced to respond to those who criticised the way Frankel was being campaigned as a four-year-old.

Grimthorpe said: 'It's not the Pony Club and you can't go for every egg-and-spoon race around. Most horses have a prep race in a Group 2 or Group 3, but Frankel went straight for the Lockinge which was of course a Group 1. The Queen Anne was a Group 1, and as Henry was keen to get another race in before York we went for the Sussex,

Sir Henry Cecil keeps a watchful eye on Frankel at York

which is another Group 1. We haven't kept his schedule secret, everyone was welcome to take him on.

'We appreciate people are so interested in him and we've had all sorts of suggestions as to what we should run him in from the July Cup to the Melbourne Cup and plenty of other weird races in between. The Juddmonte is something different as it will be his first run at a mile and a quarter. He's in very good shape after his race at Goodwood, everyone is very happy with him and he's all set for York.

'The decision as to which race he contests on Champions Day won't be made until much nearer the time. Much will depend on how he gets on in the Juddmonte.'

Ten days before York Frankel returned to Newmarket Heath when he covered a mile on the Limekilns round gallop looking as though he had fully recovered from his Goodwood exertions.

To put the critics in their place Excelebration – who had been beaten by Frankel five times during his career – landed the Group 1 Prix Jacques le Marois at Deauville, *beating a field which contained the all-aged winners of 13 previous Group 1s. This was some compliment to Frankel.*

Frankel worked again a week before York as the field began to take shape with Farhh, who had been runner-up in the Sussex Stakes, four-time Group 1 winner St Nicholas Abbey, and the previous year's International hero and Frankel's stablemate Twice Over all expected to be in opposition.

One horse who would not be taking on Frankel was Nathaniel after trainer John Gosden revealed that the King George VI and Queen Elizabeth Stakes and Coral-Eclipse scorer would go to the Irish Champion Stakes instead.

On the morning of the International Stakes the Racing Post *splashed with 'FRANKEL: THE FINAL FRONTIER. The world's best horse boldly goes where he's never gone before as he steps up to ten furlongs in the Juddmonte International'.*

Jon Lees *described yet another astonishing day.*

Frankel shows his rivals no mercy

From the sublime to the ridiculously sublime. Raising the bar lifted the amazing Frankel to even greater heights at York yesterday, as the world champion racehorse completed the transition from a mile to ten and a half furlongs in effortless fashion.

Frankel first, the rest nowhere

With every vantage point on the Knavesmire taken for the appearance of a superstar and spectators packed tens deep around the parade ring for a glimpse of a unique horse, Frankel delivered the performance a record Juddmonte International day crowd of more than 30,000 had come to witness.

Out of his comfort zone at a mile where Frankel was untouchable and into unchartered territory, the outcome was still the same – Frankel first, the rest nowhere.

This was a race Sir Henry Cecil and owner Khalid Abdulla – both absent from Frankel's Sussex Stakes victory at Glorious Goodwood – decided they couldn't miss.

There was little prospect their efforts to be on track would go unrewarded, but in the race in which Brigadier Gerard was victim of one of the greatest shocks in racing history 40 years earlier, Frankel proved its description as the graveyard of champions was dead and buried.

Settled towards the rear of the field as Robin Hood and Windsor Palace set the fractions, Frankel was able to cover St Nicholas Abbey's move two furlongs out while still on the bridle and, once let loose by Tom Queally, quickened away in a matter of strides, putting seven lengths between himself and the field.

He was cheered throughout the final furlong as Farhh sealed the runner-up spot in a photo from St Nicholas Abbey and again back in the winner's enclosure, where the crowd gave three cheers to both horse and an overwhelmed Cecil.

Queally said: 'This was some performance, because people forget how good St Nicholas Abbey is. It puts everything into context, it really paints a picture of what type of animal we're dealing with.

'He's not even gone yet and I'm missing him. He's been an amazing part of my career and everything I do from now on will be an anti-climax. I'm not a showman – I don't like all that waving and cheering but it's a job that has to be done. Words don't describe what we're dealing with – it's unbelievable.'

In the briefest of interviews with Channel 4, Cecil said the victory had made him feel '20 years better'. He added: 'It was great. It's fantastic, great for Yorkshire, great for supporters of racing.'

The way Frankel mastered his new discipline inevitably led to conjecture he could tackle 1m4f in the Prix de l'Arc de Triomphe, for which he received a 1-4 quote from Coral and William Hill and 1-2 from Ladbrokes and bet365, but although the race will be discussed, Abdulla sounded lukewarm.

'I don't think so,' he said. 'I will consult with Henry. If he thinks so we will take him. I will discuss it.'

The more likely destination for Frankel is the Qipco Champion Stakes, for which he is 1-10 with Coral to extend his perfect record to 14 wins from 14 races.

Abdulla's racing manager Teddy Grimthorpe said: 'Frankel was absolutely fantastic. The brilliant crowd absolutely appreciated him and for the horse to perform like he did is a dream.

'We are living the dream. You get so spoiled that you expect this from him. I don't want to sound arrogant at all because the way he has come through and done everything is so wonderful. The expectations are just enormous, but the fact is he keeps delivering time and time again. Each time he runs we say, 'That was amazing', then the next time, 'That was fantastic'. That is Frankel. I've never seen anything like him.'

He added: 'John Magnier came up to me beforehand and said, "This is what we are going to do. Our two boys will go on and St Nicholas Abbey will follow." There would

I'm pleased I've seen him because I'll never see another one like him.

He's an exceptional horse. I don't think I or anybody else here today will see a horse like him in our lifetime. It's an absolute honour and privilege to see him.

He's just different. He's not like a racehorse. He's more like a machine.

Fabulous, fabulous, fabulous. I'm delighted for Prince Khalid, who is such a wonderful supporter of world racing – nobody deserves a horse like him more than Prince Khalid.

Frankel was fantastic. I have never experienced anything like that at a race meeting. Well done to all involved.

No shock there then – the best racehorse in the world has won again. Well done Tom Queally and more importantly Sir Henry Cecil.

be no funny business, he said, and I said we certainly didn't expect that but thank you – the race panned out as we hoped it would.

'The plan was always Ascot and it's just a question of where we go from here. There is the Moulin – we have talked about that before. There is the Champion Stakes, there's the QEII, there's a race called the Prix de l'Arc de Triomphe, which he's not entered in.

'We have to give that some consideration but, as Henry said, the horse will tell us where we're going. Prince Khalid loves the Breeders' Cup and we would love to take Frankel to Santa Anita, Bobby Frankel's home town – the emotional ties would be fantastic.

'But unfortunately the right race is not there – we are not going to race him on dirt. It's a pity, because if they had Polytrack we'd have been there.'

Cue **Alastair Down**.

It lies in the power of the remarkable to transport us to extraordinary places, and on an indelible afternoon at York yesterday Frankel surged to fresh heights of imperiousness with a seven-length eclipse of his Juddmonte International rivals.

This was Frankel's first appearance north of Newmarket since September 2010 when he wasn't even a household name at Warren Place and sauntered home to win by 13 lengths at Doncaster on his second start as a two-year-old. The diamond still lay in the rough back then before the faultless hands of Sir Henry Cecil and his team had begun to cut and polish him to the perfection of his pre-eminence now.

Down south Frankel has put a handful of thousands on the gate at Newbury, but they do things differently in Yorkshire and for his last northern hurrah the public came to see him yesterday. And my god how they came.

From wold and dale and moor, from cities built on wool and steel, from market town and modern urban sprawl they made their way to the Knavesmire to see the equine phenomenon of our time and all our forefather's times.

Never outside of a high summer Saturday have I seen such a press of humanity on the Knavesmire with the official attendance up by a staggering 50 per cent on last year. And folk came from all over the north because there was a sight to see in Frankel. But what gave yesterday its strong, painful

Tom Queally parades Frankel in front of the packed stands

twinge of elegy was that many came also to see Cecil, an honorary Yorkshireman with deep roots up here.

Henry's father-in-law Noel Murless owned the Cliff Stud near Helmsley and his brother David ran it for years. The county is in Cecil's soul which was why he was so determined to be here, not just because this was Frankel's first foray into unknown territory, or even because the Juddmonte is his owner's very own race but because this week is the apogee of racing in Yorkshire and Henry would always want to play his part in that.

York has been one of Cecil's stamping grounds and if the foot does not hit the ground with all the ferocity of old all the fighting spirit is still evident. When his name was called to go up and receive his winner's trophy he was offered the walking stick that had been at his side throughout the afternoon.

For a second he hesitated, then smiled, shook his head and strode to the rostrum stickless and proud. And in that moment he needed no extra support other than that you could almost feel flowing out from the thousands crammed round the winner's enclosure to see a horse in a million

Tom Queally beams with delight

and his trainer of whom it is fair to say that you don't get many to the pound.

The exact severity of Cecil's illness is his business and that of those closest to his heart. He looked frail, the decidedly dodgy mafioso's black hat was new, as was the stick. His voice was a whispering husk of the usual elegant tones, but his smile was as disarming as ever and his affection for the horse that has rendered our times so memorable as strong as ever. And as he fussed over him the three cheers for the pair of them rang round an emotional winner's enclosure where the twin forces of sadness and joy were both on hand.

But never underestimate Henry's toughness or his will. He confesses to being a ferocious competitor and there is more fight in him than a dozen commandos. He was lauded everywhere he went yesterday and if the crowd's feelings could have helped him he would have been borne aloft in a sedan chair powered by pure goodwill.

And what about Frankel? Well, he was mighty here, high and mighty and almost inexplicably brilliant like some new wonder of the world.

Ridden almost like an ordinary horse for once, Tom Queally dropped him in safely out of any traffic and he travelled with an almost ludicrous ease off a serious mile-and-a-quarter pace.

And when Queally rang the telegraph to 'all ahead full' he stormed away in a manner that provoked all the usual awe plus a little bit of embarrassment for the poor old leaden-foots toiling in the white water of his wake.

I am not sure I have seen him better and the wonder does not diminish with the passing of time or the racking up of seemingly endless wins. This is a familiarity that will never know contempt. There were many on course

Frankel returns to the York winner's enclosure

yesterday who were seeing Frankel for the first time, witnessing the legend made flesh.

They now swell the ranks of folk whose racing lives have been powered by the pulse of Frankel. A happy generation that will recount its tales until the eyes of their grandchildren glaze over and they say for the umpteenth: 'He can't have been that good!'

Ah, but he is.

And the eyewitness evidence that this had been something quite exceptional was underlined by **Dave Edwards** *in his Topspeed column.*

Frankel's time performance on the Knavesmire warranted the highest speed rating ever attained in over 30 years of timekeeping by yours truly. In a contest run at a relatively even tempo he appeared to be in his comfort zone throughout and although famed for his back-to-back 10.5 second splits such wondrous feats were not needed on this occasion.

The Turftrax data reveals that with five furlongs to travel Frankel (80.65 seconds) was seventh of the nine runners, 1.38 seconds behind the leader Robin Hood. Half a mile from home he produced splits of 11.34, 11.05, 11.45 and 12.10 and soon had win number 13 in the bag. Using this time-piece as an impartial measure of excellence his speed rating of 136 put him firmly at the top of the all-time pecking order.

THE RESULT

5490 JUDDMONTE INTERNATIONAL STKS (BRITISH CHAMPIONS SERIES) (GROUP 1) **1m 2f 88y**

3:40 (3:41) (Class 1) 3-Y-O+

£411,147 (£155,875; £78,010; £38,860; £19,502; £9,787) **Stalls** Low

Form						RPR
-111	1		**Frankel**[21] 4699 4-9-5 140 .... TomQueally 7			142+
			(Sir Henry Cecil) *dwlt: hld up in rr: smooth hdwy on wd outside over 3f out: led over 2f out: shkn up and wnt clr over 1f out: impressive*		**1/10**[1]	
1322	2	7	**Farhh**[21] 4699 4-9-5 122 .... FrankieDettori 4			126
			(Saeed Bin Suroor) *trckd ldrs: hdwy over 3f out: chsng ldrs over 2f out: kpt on to take 2nd nr fin*		**10/1**[3]	
2213	3	nse	**St Nicholas Abbey (IRE)**[32] 4322 5-9-5 124 .... JPO'Brien 3			126
			(A P O'Brien, Ire) *trckd ldng trio: led briefly wl over 2f out: sn hdd: kpt on same pce over 1f out*		**5/1**[2]	
-233	4	6	**Twice Over**[46] 3880 7-9-5 118 .... IanMongan 9			114
			(Sir Henry Cecil) *hld up in rr: hdwy over 3f out: kpt on same pce to take modest 4th ins fnl f*		**12/1**	
-464	5	nk	**Bullet Train**[21] 4699 5-9-5 108 .... EddieAhern 6			113
			(Sir Henry Cecil) *led 1f: chsd ldng pair: one pce fnl 3f*		**50/1**	
6501	6	2	**Sri Putra**[25] 4610 6-9-5 116 .... (b) NeilCallan 2			109
			(Roger Varian) *hld up towards rr: effrt over 3f out: one pce fnl 2f*		**20/1**	
-330	7	3¾	**Planteur (IRE)**[63] 3267 5-9-5 117 .... WilliamBuick 8			102
			(Marco Botti) *hld up in rr: drvn over 3f out: hmpd over 2f out: wknd over 1f out*		**25/1**	
3600	8	15	**Robin Hood (IRE)**[32] 4322 4-9-5 99 .... (v) SeamieHeffernan 5			72
			(A P O'Brien, Ire) *led after 1f: hdd wl over 2f out: sn lost pl and bhd*		**100/1**	
6545	9	11	**Windsor Palace (IRE)**[27] 4521 7-9-5 106 .... (v) CO'Donoghue 1			50
			(A P O'Brien, Ire) *chsd ldr after 1f: rdn 3f out: sn edgd rt and lost pl*		**100/1**	

2m 6.6s (-5.91) **Going Correction** -0.025s/f (Good) **9** Ran SP% **136.9**

Speed ratings (Par 117): **122,116,116,111,111 109,106,94,85**

Tote Swingers: 1&2 £1.80, 1&3 £1.60, 2&3 £2.20 CSF £4.18 TOTE £1.10: £1.02, £2.40, £1.30; EX 4.30 Trifecta £8.90 Pool: £26,193.49 - 2,168.11 winning units..

Owner K Abdulla **Bred** Juddmonte Farms Ltd **Trained** Newmarket, Suffolk

■ Stewards' Enquiry : Eddie Ahern four-day ban: used whip above permitted level (Sep 5-7,9)

Analysis

GRAHAM DENCH

A new challenge at last, and one of the defining performances of Frankel's career.

While those closest to him never had the slightest doubt that he would stay the longer trip, he still had to prove it, and the opposition was stronger than many expected, with St Nicholas Abbey a four-time Group 1 winner, including at the Breeders' Cup, his own stablemate Twice Over a previous Juddmonte winner and also successful in two Champion Stakes and an Eclipse, Planteur successful in a Prix Ganay, Sri Putra another solid international yardstick, and Sussex second Farhh open to improvement back up in trip.

St Nicholas Abbey's two pacemakers set a pace guaranteed to expose any flaws in Frankel's stamina, but Queally rode with complete confidence once again and was vindicated when Frankel cruised to the front in breathtaking fashion around two out, nearest the stands' rail after the entire field tacked over, and then quickened away as brilliantly as he ever had at a mile.

Despite the longer trip and strong pace, it yet again took Queally an age to pull up, suggesting that a mile and a half would be no problem if required.

4.05
RACE 5

Qipco Champion Stakes (British Champions Middle Distance) (Group 1) (Class 1) BBC1

Winner £737,230

1m2f

£1,300,000 guaranteed **For** 3yo+ **Weights** 3yo colts and geldings 8st 12lb; fillies 8st 9lb 4yo+ colts and geldings 9st 3lb; fillies 9st **Weight for age** 3 from 4yo+ 5lb **Entries** 46 pay £4550 **1st Forfeit** 17 pay £4225 **Confirmed** 8 pay £4225 **Penalty value 1st** £737,230 **2nd** £279,500 **3rd** £139,880 **4th** £69,680 **5th** £34,970 **6th** £17,550 **Tariff** £160,000

1 (4)	78-4645 **BULLET TRAIN** [59] *b h Sadler's Wells-Kind* **Sir Henry Cecil** K Abdulla	5 9-3 Ian Mongan	(124)
2 (1)	5-2112d1 **CIRRUS DES AIGLES** (FR) TTF[14] **D**8 **CD**1 *b g Even Top-Taille de Guepe* **Mme C Barande-Barbe** (FR) Jean-Claude-Alain Dupouy	6 9-3 Olivier Peslier	(142)
3 (3)	11-1111 **FRANKEL** TTF[59] **D**1 **C**4 *b c Galileo-Kind* **Sir Henry Cecil** K Abdulla	4 9-3 Tom Queally	(153)
4 (2)	-233181 **MASTER OF HOUNDS** (USA) [48] *b c Kingmambo-Silk And Scarlet* **William Haggas**[2] Sheikh Mohammed Bin Khalifa Al Maktoum	4 9-3 Ryan Moore	(126)
5 (6)	115-122 **NATHANIEL** (IRE) TTF[42] **BF D**1 **C**2 *b c Galileo-Magnificient Style* **John Gosden** Lady Rothschild & Newsells Park Stud	4 9-3 William Buick	(138)
6 (5)	-471131 **PASTORIUS** (GER) [17] **D**2 *b c Soldier Hollow-Princess Li* **Mario Hofer** (GER) Stall Antanando	3 8-12 Frankie Dettori	(133)

2011 (12 ran) Cirrus Des Aigles (1) Mme C Barande-Barbe 5 9-3 12/1 Christophe Soumillon
RPR130

BETTING FORECAST: 1-5 Frankel, 4 Cirrus Des Aigles, 10 Nathaniel, 33 Pastorius, 100 Master Of Hounds, 250 Bullet Train.

QIPCO Champion Stakes

Ascot, October 20, 2012

At the start of September it was announced that Frankel would race in the Qipco Champion Stakes on British Champions Day on October 20. The other options of the Breeders' Cup and the Prix de l'Arc de Triomphe were discounted, but the decision to choose Ascot was a coup for the royal racecourse.

Ascot head of PR Nick Smith said: 'It's not entirely unexpected because we were always the front-runner, but to have it confirmed, and have it confirmed early enough to promote, is extremely helpful.

Frankel (right) works with Bullet Train on the Watered Gallop on Wednesday, September 19, 2012

*Sir Henry Cecil gives
Tom Queally his instructions
before the Rowley Mile gallop*

'The Frankel factor is going to sell tickets quicker and we
will have to sit down next week and think about whether to
raise our capacity. Our nominal capacity is 30,000, but we
would hope we can increase that and be prepared to push
towards 35,000. We are getting to the stage where Premier
admission will almost certainly sell out next week.'

A week later Frankel returned to work for the first
time since York when he breezed over seven furlongs on
the Al Bahathri Polytrack with regular work companion
Bullet Train, after which Cecil said: 'Frankel seems to be
in the form of his life at present. He was a bit fresh just
after York but he is fine again now and moved beautifully
this morning.'

Following the previously trodden path, Cecil revealed
that Frankel would have a gallop on the Rowley Mile
before racing on Cambridgeshire day at Newmarket at the
end of September. **Lee Mottershead** was there to witness
this workout:

The victory was achieved with ridiculous ease, complete
nonchalance and a delicious slice of arrogance. You could
point out that it was only a racecourse gallop, but in most
of his races Frankel has been required to exert not an
ounce more energy than was needed here.

They packed themselves deep around the pre-parade
ring and then the paddock before filling the stands for the

race that took place before the racing. As expected, the outcome was a one-two-three for Sir Henry Cecil and the right horse won in the manner everyone expected. In literal terms it was non-event, yet at the same time it was an occasion to be savoured, for now there is only Ascot.

Specific Gravity, loaned for the afternoon by the Niarchos family, set off in front, followed by Frankel's usual pacemaker Bullet Train and then the latter's rather more talented younger brother, partnered, as ever, by Tom Queally. Around three furlongs from home, Bullet Train took over, then a furlong later the inevitable happened and by many lengths.

'We're all very disappointed because we've backed the Niarchos horse,' joked Khalid Abdulla's racing manager Teddy Grimthorpe, who unsurprisingly stated connections were more than satisfied.

'He's done everything we hoped he would do,' he said. 'He's done it with the minimum fuss, as he usually does. It was about keeping him lean and mean and he's been reminded he still has work to do.

'The whole idea was to give him a little bit extra than he would have got in a normal workout. It's achieved that, and isn't it amazing how many people have come out to see him?' Cecil, voice still weak due to ongoing cancer treatment, was given the opportunity to decline an interview but chose not to. He wanted to talk about Frankel and, when doing so, made clear this had been preferable to running 13 days ago in the Prix du Moulin.

'I don't think that would have achieved anything,' he said. 'I think this was a better idea. He had a nice blow, but I wanted him to because this is not D-Day.'

That day is October 20 when the unbeaten world champion bids for his 14th – and almost certainly his final – success in the Qipco Champion Stakes, for which he is 1-12 with Coral.

'It's for Prince Khalid to say when the curtain comes down, but it's likely to be at Ascot,' confirmed Grimthorpe. 'As far as I know, we're not suddenly going to jump out and say we're going to this, that or the other. We've had three fantastic years and if people haven't made up their minds about him by now they haven't been watching the same races I have.'

And this was our penultimate chance to watch a thoroughbred who is just 4-1 with William Hill to sire a 2017 Classic winner from his first crop. Seeing him delighted the 8,510 crowd – up 18 per cent – but they were also thrilled to see Cecil, who used his appearance to underline that although Frankel's career is about to finish his is not.

'I'm going fine,' he said. 'I read somebody said I'm going to retire. The only retiring I'm going to do is have a good holiday. I'm all right. I'm going well.'

As, with three weeks to go until Frankel's farewell appearance, is the horse of Cecil's lifetime and our's.

The prep work for his final start continued as the make-up of the Champion Stakes field began to take shape with 2011 hero Cirrus Des Aigles returning from a long absence to win at Longchamp on Arc weekend and John Gosden preparing Nathaniel for the race. With Frankel beating Nathaniel on their debuts at Newmarket in August 2010 – since when Nathaniel had won the 2011 King George VI and Queen Elizabeth Stakes and 2012 Eclipse Stakes, and had been narrowly beaten in the King George the same year – it would be a wonderful piece of symmetry for these horses to face one another on their final starts.

Frankel had a final workout on the Al Bahathri Polytrack on the Tuesday before Champions Day, and Sir Henry Cecil believed he could be even better on soft ground, as the rain continued to fall at Ascot.

Peter Thomas *talked to the gallop-watchers who had became used to seeing Frankel on the Heath and whose morning would become a little less bright after his final start:*

It's a normal Monday on Warren Hill with the normal air of a weekend just gone and another brewing in the near distance. Except that this weekend will be anything but normal.

On Saturday, Frankel, the best racehorse in the world, will be running his last race, which means that the imposing figure now cantering towards us will, after another couple of days of routine exercise, be seen no more on the Heath of a morning.

Those who have come to view the presence of greatness as a matter of routine will be shaken from their complacency and forced to peer into the gaping rent left in the fabric of the racing community as the star of Headquarters 'leaves the building' for the final time. No longer will the second horse in Sir Henry Cecil's string, following hard on the heels of Bullet Train, be the unbeaten Frankel, ridden by Shane Fetherstonhaugh in a fluorescent yellow vest.

Cecil's wife Jane sums it up as she oversees the canter that leads inexorably towards this weekend's last hurrah. 'In some ways it can't come quick enough and in other ways it'll be very hard when it happens,' she says. 'Everyone knows he's always at the front of the string and it's going to be strange for those of us who are out here every day when he's not up there any more.'

Even a seasoned professional like the Post's own Newmarket gallops man David Milnes, a Frankel watcher from day one, admits to a sense of foreboding as he waits for the seismic shift in what has established itself as the world order.

'He's been a great feature of my life for the last three seasons,' says Milnes, snapping a few final pictures of the mighty beast on his mobile phone, 'and it's sad it's coming to a close. It probably won't sink in until next spring when he's not there doing his usual canters up Warren Hill. Now it's easy to think he's just going away for the winter, but come February or March we'll really miss him.

'The first time I saw Frankel he got off the box and we all thought he was Bullet Train because he was such a physically well-developed two-year-old. The great thing about him is that he's a horse who has always done it on the gallops as well as on the track, which from my point of view makes it far easier and far more rewarding.

'Some of his work has been stunning – the only one to come close was Dubai Millennium – and I remember before the Dewhurst, when Dream Ahead was going to go up against Frankel, Dave Simcock was standing on Racecourse Side waiting for his horses to come up and it so happened that Frankel was coming around at the same time. Frankel just about took his nose off as he went past and Dave was open-mouthed – he knew he was staring down the barrel from then on.

'I've had to be on the ball with a horse like him – it's been very important to be extra-vigilant, but at least you don't have to try too hard when you've got that much material. I don't think we've got anything to replace him at the moment.'

Cecil's fellow trainers stress that on the gallops Frankel is just another horse taking his turn on the communal facilities, although some have been known to steady their strings to make way for the champion.

Others, meanwhile, claim to have opted for a less polite approach. 'I don't get out of his way,' says Hugo Palmer, 'I try to get my fillies in front of him to increase their value!'

But while Palmer tries to make the most of Frankel's last days at work, others are resigned to the inevitable and seeking the positives.

'I always feel with horses like that you're lucky to have had them,' says John Gosden. 'It's been a pleasure being out watching him work all the time and of course it will leave a hole, but with a bit of luck he's only going to be a mile and a half over the hill at Banstead Manor Stud for everyone to go and see him – and I'm sure they'll wear a path to his box.'

Simcock is another to point out the lift that Frankel has given to the entire Newmarket community, just by being there. 'We all have our own to concentrate on,' he says, 'but we all recognise we'll be lucky if we ever see another one like him. We all love reading about him and the great thing is that there's no jealousy surrounding a horse like him – everybody loves a star.'

His thoughts are echoed by Nick Patton, who as training grounds manager for Jockey Club Estates has found his working life enriched by the showstopping four-year-old and who envisages a fitting recognition of his achievements.

'I've seen masses of him on a daily basis and it'll leave a bit of a hole when he's gone, but that's the great thing about this sport – everybody's ready for the next one.

'He's had no preferential treatment from JCE, which is credit to Sir Henry, but after he's gone I'm sure we'll all sit down and appreciate how phenomenal a racehorse he's been.

'He's the greatest and to have the greatest trained in Newmarket has been wonderful for everybody.

'I think we should celebrate our champions a little more and that's one of the things the town council is looking to do, to create a Legends of the Turf walk in the paving stones, Hollywood style, and if that happened I think Frankel would be the first one to go in there.'

For everybody in racing, Frankel's retirement will be a disappointment, but for those in Newmarket it will be felt more immediately. For all at Warren Place there is a tearful moment on its way, as trainer Michael Bell explains.

JOHNNY MURTAGH
jockey

The immortal Frankel! The best we've seen, well done to all at Warren Place

GRAEME MCDOWELL
golfer

I once had a car that couldn't go as fast as #Frankel #1994nissanaltima

PETER CHAPPLE-HYAM
trainer

Smoked more fags, shouted more than any runner I've ever had. Frankel supreme. No need say more. Sir Henry simply the best. TQ quality

CLARE BALDING
broadcaster

Well that was all rather emotional. He's retired with the perfect record and he's the best we've ever seen. #Frankel

JAMIE SPENCER
jockey

Great day for Frankel. Queally was class on him from a jockey perspective, no jockey could've been more helpful to the horse

SUZI PERRY
broadcaster

To stop any squabbling at the @bbcsport personality of the year, shall we just award #Frankel? 100% superstar

'The real wrench will be when the time comes for him to leave the yard for the last time. There were two things in my life that I couldn't bring myself to do: the first was to take my daughter off to boarding school and the second was to put Pass The Peace, my first really good horse, on the box when she left us. I bottled both and Mrs Bell had to do them.'

Another good thing is about to come to an end, as good things must, and Newmarket will be the poorer for it. But with the end of Frankel, however sad that may be, comes the beginning of the search for the new Frankel.

The following day there was morning exercise with a difference for the Household Cavalry Mounted Regiment when they stepped out from Hyde Park Barracks in London.

Eighteen members of the regiment paraded in the pink, green and white colours of Frankel in celebration of his final career start at Ascot.

Meanwhile the rain continued to fall at Ascot and there was some discussion about whether Frankel would run if conditions were very testing, but after walking the course on the morning of the race Teddy Grimthorpe announced that Frankel would take part. Everyone was thrilled that he did, and **Jon Lees** *was there to see a perfect ending for a perfect racehorse:*

Frankel's greatness was for once measured not by a winning distance but a winning performance yesterday as the turf's world champion overcame slow ground and a slow start to sign off a perfect career before a rapturous and adoring public.

Only rock stars are afforded the kind of ovation Frankel and Sir Henry Cecil received yesterday at Ascot where a sellout 32,000 crowd witnessed an extraordinary career climax in a defining encounter for the Qipco Champion Stakes.

British Champions Day's headline act put an unbeaten record of 13 straight victories on the line against a field containing two of the world's other top six turf horses on going he was not certain to act on and still emerged top of the bill, stretching his sequence to 14 with the dismissal of Cirrus Des Aigles and Nathaniel.

Cecil, trainer of numerous other champions, has always left it for others to judge Frankel, but after witnessing this final effort he was unequivocal. Battling stomach cancer

Members of the Household Cavalry Mounted Regiment parade in the pink, green and white colours of Frankel, Wednesday, October 17, 2012

and his voice barely a whisper, Cecil said: 'He's the best I've ever had, the best I've ever seen. I'd be very surprised if there's ever been a better horse.'

After three seasons in which Frankel has been champion, owner Khalid Abdulla said there was nothing left for the horse to prove. 'That is the end,' he said. 'He will be retired. I think he would have been further in front of the others if it hadn't been for the ground.'

A wet week had given rise to speculation that Frankel might not run or at least not be at his best against last year's Champion Stakes winner Cirrus Des Aigles and Eclipse and King George VI and Queen Elizabeth Stakes victor Nathaniel, who were both proven on the surface, but Abdulla's racing manager Teddy Grimthorpe was quite happy with conditions when he walked the course in the morning.

Of more concern was the way Frankel flopped out of the stalls at the start to concede a few lengths to the field, leaving Ian Mongan to restrain pacemaker Bullet Train and look back to see where the stablemate and Tom Queally were.

Frankel made up the ground and Bullet Train went on from five furlongs out until Olivier Peslier on Cirrus Des Aigles retook the advantage with well over two furlongs to run. But then Frankel ranged upside a furlong out and, once shaken up, stretched out to get home by a length and three-quarters with Nathaniel two and a half lengths further back. Cecil said: 'He was labouring on the ground and not happy on it, but he was very relaxed throughout. I have probably got him too relaxed, it used to be the other way. In the end he had plenty in hand.

'I cannot believe in the history of racing there has ever been a better horse. I have enjoyed every moment of training him, although it has been slightly stressful at times.'

Frankel's victory triggered a stampede from the stands to the parade ring where the crowds strained to see the great colt. They were kept waiting as Queally paraded his mount before an appreciative audience.

'The crowd was larger at Royal Ascot but it was more intense today,' said Queally. 'It was like a bigger thing waiting to explode, and I don't know where I'd have gone if I hadn't won.

'I was a little worried about the conditions, but having walked the track the home straight wasn't too heavy.

'He is better on better ground. You don't see Formula One cars winning on anything other than tarmac so for him to go and do that goes to show what sort of horse he is. We'll never see another like him. I went down an extra hundred yards to let the crowd soak it all in. It meant I could spend an extra 20 seconds on the track.'

Grimthorpe said there was never any real doubt about Frankel running. 'Henry was insistent he was going to run,' he said. 'There was endless rain coming and people were ringing saying it was going to be Swinley bottomless, as I call it, but when I walked it this morning it was soft and heavy in that bottom area but the old mile and straight was more than acceptable.

'Frankel has given us three sensational years and been a champion at two, three and four. If you haven't made your mind up about him now, I don't think you've been watching.

'Henry's handling of him proved he is the master of his profession. Henry on his own is incredibly determined and his re-emergence as a top-flight trainer is one of the all-time great stories. He has come back from the Conference to top of the Champions League.'

Following spread: Frankel meets his adoring public before the Qipco Champion Stakes

Cirrus Des Aigles's trainer Corine Barande-Barbe said: 'It is not a dishonour to be beaten by such a good horse. I don't think they went overly fast and that did not help, but no excuses – Frankel is the best.'

Nathaniel also retires to stud, and his trainer John Gosden said: 'Nathaniel has done everything, a mile and a quarter and a mile and a half, fast ground, soft ground. He's run a great race and had a great season.'

David Milnes *spoke at Ascot to the Cecil backroom team, who had a nervous moment before cheering their hero home:*

Sir Henry Cecil's backroom staff were full of emotion as they watched their superstar's curtain call in the Qipco Champion Stakes, with assistant trainer Mike Marshall, farrier Stephen Kielt and Frankel's work-rider Shane Fetherstonhaugh among the throng.

Hot-footing it from escorting Frankel out on to the track, Marshall joined his wife Aideen in a packed owners' and trainers' stand to view the action. Things got off to a nervous start when their hero missed the break. 'He's lazy. But lazy is good, leave him there,' offered Aideen.

As Tom Queally made a mid-race move to get close to Nathaniel, Marshall observed: 'Tom has got to be happy the way he is travelling.'

As Frankel swung into the straight and ranged up to Cirrus Des Aigles, the place erupted. 'Go on Tom, go on Tom,' chorused the Marshalls, a cry that continued after the superstar had crossed the line in glory.

After a celebratory hug, it was back to the day job for Marshall to shadow the legend back into the winner's enclosure, where the joint was jumping.

Afterwards Fetherstonhaugh, who has played a key role in harnessing Frankel's power on the gallops, was in tears in the paddock. He said: 'I can't go through that again – that's the hardest thing I've ever watched.

'He showed different qualities today, like how tough he is. I thought that was the best he has ever gone to post and he just fell out of the stalls, but he showed his class when it mattered.'

Kielt said: 'My reaction is one of relief. He didn't like the ground but he did what he was asked to do.'

Frankel's groom Sandeep Gauravaram said: 'He fell out of the stalls a little, but when Tom came there two out

Frankel makes it 14 out of 14, with Cirrus Des Aigles and Nathaniel well beaten off

on the bridle I knew he would get there as he was in very good form.'

As to the future, he added: 'I won't see his like again and he is a legend back home in India. I thought he was good today but I still think his 2,000 Guineas victory was his most impressive.'

Down at the start with Frankel, as usual, was equine guru and stalls expert Steve 'Yarmy' Dyble. He joked: 'Frankel got left a little bit at the start. I think he might have to have a stalls test if he runs again!'

More seriously he added: 'Shane's done a great job settling the horse down and deserves a lot of credit. He doesn't really need me at the start – it's all about him.'

Alastair Down *witnessed a day of raw emotion in which a unique legend of the Turf wrote his final chapter:*

On an imperishable Ascot afternoon marbled through with emotion, the unbeaten force of thoroughbred nature that has been Frankel took his leave of us lesser creatures yesterday and now passes from our sight with his place in turf myth and legend forever assured.

My hero: an emotional Tom Queally shows Frankel how much he means to him

And for all his 14 victories and nine consecutive Group 1s, Frankel has long ceased to be about facts and figures. The public's relationship with this unsurpassable horse has become a matter of the heart and, believe me, there were tears speckling the cheers because there is something almost inexplicably humbling about being in the presence of greatness of this magnitude.

We know we have never seen the likes of him and are all but certain that no members of preceding racing generations have either, and watching him and that genius Sir Henry Cecil yesterday just made you grateful to your very marrow that their time has also been your time.

And this victory was no bloodless cakewalk. We knew the ground was a threat and that in Cirrus Des Aigles he faced a battle-hardened campaigner who would have to be carried out on his shield in order to be beaten.

And then when the stalls crashed open, there he wasn't. Frankel fell out of the stalls losing a good three lengths and, with pacemaking plans suddenly in a state of disarray as Ian Mongan on Bullet Train looked round to locate his workmate, there were several furlongs of anxiety that this race had all the makings of going wrong on us all.

But to his undying credit Tom Queally never panicked or made any knee-jerk move that might have lit Frankel up mid-race. He turned into Ascot's short straight in fourth and from that moment, until some 20 minutes later when he completed his second lap of honour round the paddock, Ascot racecourse took flight into zones of excitement and sheer joy such as I have never before had the privilege of witnessing on the Flat.

As Frankel answered Queally's questions for the 14th and final time, the crowd sensed that this was not yet in the bag and 32,000 voices were raised as one as they bayed their encouragement to the pink and green.

There was an urgency to the roar and the myriad prayers were answered as Frankel lowered that fine head and began to chew into the leeway.

Cirrus Des Aigles is not the faltering type, but he had no answer to the irresistible force in pursuit of him and when the favourite hit the front, battle standard flying, with just over a furlong to run the noise hit a never-to-be-forgotten crescendo as everyone realised that their most heartfelt hopes were coming to a climax before their very eyes.

Queally had to resort to the whip in the final 100 yards but by then the day was won and when he brought Frankel back in front of the stands a couple of minutes later they were packed 20-deep down by the rails as the faithful let their gratitude rip.

And while there was a veritable bedlam of acclaim that broke out when Frankel returned to the winner's enclosure, I doubt that I was alone in feeling a touch of sadness nagging the throat as this was a valedictory day and all final goodbyes are heir to a tear.

The mind flicked back to the other days he has given us. I have seen him 12 wonderful times as he has taken his 14 leaps into immortality. The first was here in the Royal Lodge three years ago when that notable judge Jim McGrath walked back off the stands and said: 'That might be the best two-year-old I have ever seen.' Move over Nostradamus.

And what places and heights Frankel has taken us too – the raw, almost impossibly headstrong talent of this horse tamed, honed and refined by Cecil and his Warren Place team into an animal who can genuinely be described as the ultimate racehorse.

*Sir Henry Cecil and
Tom Queally enjoy the moment*

As Frankel made his way round the paddock, Cecil could suddenly be spotted entirely on his own watching his career-crowning achievement as the crowds cheered and applauded.

A man born to train a horse such as this, one wondered what was running through his mind as the day is coming when this horse will leave Warren Place and, this time, not return.

Henry accepted my thanks for the days this horse has given us and said he was 'too relaxed', but frankly that is the triumph of the way he has been trained. Shane Fetherstonhaugh has played a central role and the quiet Queally has guided him with sure hands, but Frankel has been Henry's masterpiece and, by the trainer's own admission, has been a sustaining force in his unblinking struggle with cancer.

The fight has left its marks on Henry and you ache at the attrition but, by God, he has a gladiator's courage.

And it was fitting that Frankel's last triumph should be at Ascot as Cecil has all but annexed the place down the long years of his immaculate mastery.

And now it is over – 'The tumult and the shouting dies, the captains and the kings depart'. We have had the privilege of wondrous times gifted to us by a great horse. We have witnessed things beyond the imaginings of other generations and have indeed 'Been to the mountain top and seen the Promised Land'. Adieu and amen.

THE RESULT

7239	**QIPCO CHAMPION STKS (BRITISH CHAMPIONS MIDDLE DISTANCE) (GROUP 1)**	1m 2f

4:05 (4:11) (Class 1) 3-Y-O+

£737,230 (£279,500; £139,880; £69,680; £34,970; £17,550)   **Stalls** Low

Form					RPR
1111	**1**		**Frankel**[59] [5490] 4-9-3 140.. TomQueally 3		137+
			(Sir Henry Cecil) s.s: rcvrd into 4th after 3f: brought wd and prog over 2f		
			out: cruised up to ld over 1f out: shkn up to assert fnl f	2/11[1]	
1121	**2**	1 ¾	**Cirrus Des Aigles (FR)**[14] [6898] 6-9-3 130..................... OlivierPeslier 1		133
			(Mme C Barande-Barbe, France) led after 1f to over 5f out: led again wl		
			over 2f out and kicked on: rdn and hdd over 1f out: styd on but readily		
			hld	9/2[2]	
-122	**3**	2 ½	**Nathaniel (IRE)**[42] [6063] 4-9-3 126........................... WilliamBuick 6		128
			(John Gosden) sweating: trckd ldr after 2f to 6f out: rdn to chal over 2f		
			out: btn off over 1f out: one pce	9/1[3]	
1131	**4**	3 ½	**Pastorius (GER)**[17] [6805] 3-8-12 122.......................... FrankieDettori 5		121
			(Mario Hofer, Germany) hld up in last: effrt to go 4th 2f out: no imp on ldr		
			after	33/1	
3101	**5**	4	**Master Of Hounds (USA)**[48] [5869] 4-9-3 115................... RyanMoore 2		113
			(William Haggas) hld up and sn in 5th: rdn and wknd over 2f out	80/1	
4645	**6**	2 ½	**Bullet Train**[59] [5490] 5-9-3 113............................... IanMongan 4		108
			(Sir Henry Cecil) led 1f: restrained: moved up to ld again over 5f out to wl		
			over 2f out: wknd	100/1	

2m 10.22s (2.82) **Going Correction** +0.675s/f (Yiel)

WFA 3 from 4yo+ 5lb   **6** Ran   SP% **118.0**

Speed ratings (Par 117):   **115,113,111,108,105 103**

toteswingers 1&2 £1.10, 2&3 £1.40, 1&3 £1.20 CSF £1.77 TOTE £1.30: £1.02, £2.20; EX 2.10.

Owner K Abdulla **Bred** Juddmonte Farms Ltd **Trained** Newmarket, Suffolk

FOCUS

The best Champion Stakes for many a year and a fantastic result with Frankel signing off with a perfect record. He was a little below his best on the testing ground, though.

Analysis

GRAHAM DENCH

Perhaps Frankel's toughest challenge, with ground bordering on heavy to contend with for the first time, in addition to top drawer opponents in Cirrus Des Aigles, a proven mudlover whose 16 wins included a defeat of So You Think in the corresponding race 12 months previously, and Nathaniel, who had won a King George and an Eclipse since running him close when the pair made their racecourse debuts.

Underfoot conditions were such a concern that there was even an element of doubt about Frankel's participation, and while the decision to run was vindicated in the most spellbinding fashion, events did not play out in quite the anticipated manner.

The drama began at the start, when Frankel was much more slowly away than Tom Queally intended and needed chasing into his bridle to be competitive. Frankel's slow start left Ian Mongan on Bullet Train looking anxiously over his shoulder to see where he was and reining back to try to assist, and it was not until past halfway that the pacemaker was in front again. Even then he was of no great help.

When Cirrus Des Aigles kicked on again straightening for home Frankel was widest of all with a little work to do still, but Queally had the situation in hand and concerns were largely put to rest when Frankel moved up on his two main rivals with an ease that will live long in the memory, before quickening decisively.

With the ground plainly not to Frankel's liking Queally gave him a rare smack with his left hand to settle the issue and be sure, and the winning margin was much less extravagant than usual. However, the job was done and he would retire unbeaten.

Frankel's last success was by no means his most spectacular, nor one of his best from a ratings perspective, yet the combination of class, speed, and, finally, grit with which he accomplished the most difficult of tasks encapsulated much of what made him so great.

A fitting climax to a faultless racecourse career.

The Raceform view

Graham Dench

Comparisons may be odious, but in sport they are as inevitable as they are irresistible.

Frankel's standing among the all-time greats has been the talk of racing ever since that devastating annihilation in the 2,000 Guineas, not halfway into his career, and the arguments continued to Champions Day and beyond, on the racetrack, in betting shops and on the letters pages.

Now that it is over we all have our own opinions on just where he stands, but opinions are all that they are.

In such a debate it is a source of frustration that in 14 races he was tried over such a narrow range of distances, from seven furlongs to a mile and a quarter; that he did not take either of the two definitive tests, in the Derby or the Prix de l'Arc de Triomphe; and also that he raced only in his home country.

Indeed his achievements – sublime though they are – can be trumped in at least one significant respect by every one of those who are popularly recognised as the best of modern times.

After all, Ribot was undefeated from five furlongs to just short of two miles and in three countries, counting the King George and two Prix de l'Arcs among 16 wins; Sea Bird II, beaten only once, won both the Derby and an exceptionally strong Arc with contemptuous ease; Nijinsky, the only Triple Crown winner of the period, was also a champion two-year-old; Brigadier Gerard, although never campaigned abroad, was a Group 1 winner from six furlongs to a mile and a half and was beaten only once in 18 starts; Mill Reef, although no match for Brigadier Gerard the one time they met, was a spectacular two-year-old and an impressive winner of both the Derby and the Arc; Dancing Brave won the Guineas and the Arc, and he should have won the Derby too; Sea The Stars won the 2,000 Guineas, Derby and Arc in a faultless three-year-old campaign.

But unlike most of the above, Frankel never had a simple task. He simply made them look simple as he rattled up an unprecedented tally of performances that the ratings experts all agree merited exceptional marks. And for sheer brilliance, for overwhelming superiority over contemporaries, for class, charisma and flair, he was a match for each and every one of them.

What's more, few now doubt that he would have had the speed to succeed in Group 1 sprints, the stamina to have won a Derby or an Arc, and both the constitution and the temperament to have extended his domination abroad – if only he had been given the chance.

In short, he was equine perfection – the embodiment of the consummate thoroughbred.

Nobody can prove definitively that he is the best of them all, but most of us will take a huge amount of persuading that he isn't.

Frankel's career in summary

2010

13 Aug	Newmarket	soft	European Breeders' Fund Maiden Stakes	8	T Queally	7-4F	WON	£4,533.20
10 Sept	Doncaster	good	Frank Whittle Partnership Conditions Stakes	7	T Queally	1-2F	WON	£10,904.25
25 Sept	Ascot	good to soft	Juddmonte Royal Lodge Stakes (Gp2)	8	T Queally	30-100F	WON	£70,962.50
16 Oct	Newmarket	good to soft	Dubai Dewhurst Stakes (Gp1)	7	T Queally	4-6F	WON	£180,074.44

2011

16 April	Newbury	good to firm	Totesport.com Greenham Stakes (Gp3)	7	T Queally	1-4F	WON	£28,385
30 April	Newmarket	good to firm	Qipco 2,000 Guineas (Gp1)	8	T Queally	1-2F	WON	£198,695
14 June	Ascot	good	St James's Palace Stakes (Gp1)	8	T Queally	30-100F	WON	£141,925
27 July	Goodwood	good	Qipco Sussex Stakes (Gp1)	8	T Queally	8-13F	WON	£170,130
15 Oct	Ascot	good	Queen Elizabeth II Stakes Sponsored by Qipco (Gp1)	8	T Queally	4-11F	WON	£567,100

2012

19 May	Newbury	good	JLT Lockinge Stakes (Gp1)	8	T Queally	2-7F	WON	£99,242.50
19 June	Ascot	good to soft	Queen Anne Stakes (Gp1)	8	T Queally	1-10F	WON	£198,485
1 Aug	Goodwood	good	Qipco Sussex Stakes (Gp1)	8	T Queally	1-20F	WON	£179,487.15
22 Aug	York	good to firm	Juddmonte International Stakes (Gp1)	10	T Queally	1-10F	WON	£411,147.50
20 Oct	Ascot	soft	Qipco Champion Stakes (Gp1)	10	T Queally	2-11F	WON	£737,230

LEFT TO RIGHT: date, course, going, race name (with Pattern status in parentheses); distance in furlongs; jockey; starting price; finishing position; prize-money in £ sterling

Frankel facts and figures

- Frankel raced 14 times, winning 14;
- was ridden in all his races by Tom Queally;
- ran all his races in England;
- earned £2,998,302 in prize-money;
- covered 113 furlongs in his 14 races;
- raced for 21 mins 59.80 secs;
- longest price: 7-4 on his debut in 2010;
- shortest price: 1-20 in 2012 Qipco Sussex Stakes;
- longest winning distance: 13 lengths in Frank Whittle Partnership Conditions Stakes;
- shortest winning distance: half a length in European Breeders' Fund Maiden Stakes.
- But it is the less obvious figures which proclaim the true quality of Frankel, as Topspeed's Dave Edwards explains:

Obviously there is far more to Frankel than mere numbers, but he is a time-keeper's dream, fast and furious ridden out and winning by wide margins. The initial glimpses of his extraordinary talent were evident on only his second start at Doncaster's St Leger meeting. In a three-runner race he absolutely annihilated the opposition and earned 115, the best figures on the card and no mean achievement for a juvenile.

He equalled that feat and posted an improved time-figure (124) when winning the Dewhurst at Newmarket the following month, clocking the quickest time of three races over seven furlongs.

His explosive 2,000 Guineas success (132) is unlikely ever to be matched in both style and substance, and although things did not go to plan in the St James's Palace Stakes at Royal Ascot, his class and brilliance carried him through.

In 2012 the Queen Anne turned into a rout, and his 125 was the pick of Royal Ascot; his searing pace was epitomised by his breathtaking split times as he peaked at 42.53 mph.

He earned a figure of 120 in Goodwood's Sussex Stakes and although he faced only three rivals he came home in a final quarter of 22.57 seconds and was clocked at 43.19 in the penultimate furlong.

His stunning York success, where he toyed with the opposition, and the relatively even tempo of the Juddmonte International, allowed him to attain a career-best 136 on this time-piece.

Underfoot conditions were far from ideal in Ascot's Champion Stakes, and while visually his win was not spectacular, a figure of 134 set the seal on a remarkable career.

On six occasions he has breached the 120 mark and on three occasions the 130. He has three of the four highest ever Topspeed ratings on my watch, and really was simply the best.